HEAD NASHVILLE N

R HOME **BEN RECTOR** FOGGY

R FLATT AND EARL SCRUGGS HOW

? **DR. HUMPHREY BATE AND HIS POSSUM**

ES KEEP MY SKILLET GOOD

NNESSEE HOMESICK BLUES

**LORETTA LYNN** CRAZY **PATSY CLINE**

NKY TONK ANGELS **KITTY WELLS**

AND WAIT) **LITTLE JIMMY DICKENS**

N TENNESSEE **HOMER AND JETHRO**

TUNE **BILLY EDD WHEELER** MAMA

ICKEN **TOM T. HALL** BURGERS

CAN'T HURT HAM **RICKY SKAGGS**

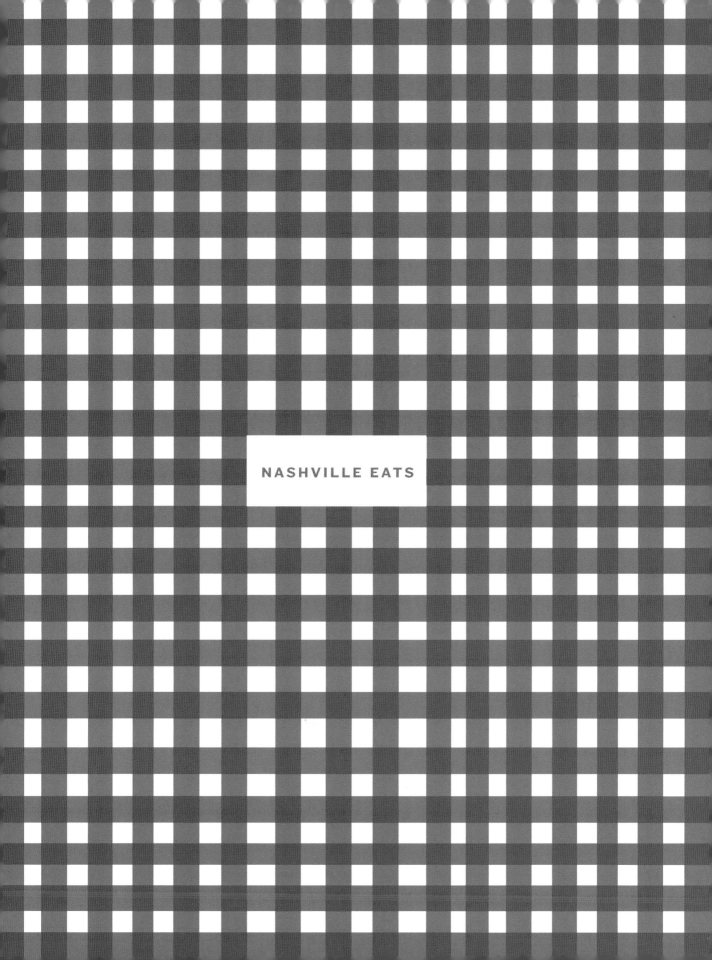

NASHVILLE EATS

Published in 2015 by Abrams

text copyright © 2015 Jennifer Justus

photographs copyright © 2015 Andrea Behrends

Library of Congress Control Number:
2014959141

ISBN: 978-1-61769-169-0

Editor: Holly Dolce
Designer: Deb Wood
Production Manager: True Sims

The text of this book was composed in
Bau, Knockout, and Mercury

Hand lettering: Norma Jeanne Maloney /
Red Rider Studios

Printed and bound in China

10 9 8

Abrams books are available at special
discounts when purchased in quantity for
premiums and promotions as well as fundraising
or educational use. Special editions can also
be created to specification. For details, contact
specialsales@abramsbooks.com or the address
below.

**ABRAMS** The Art of Books
195 Broadway, New York, NY 10007
abramsbooks.com

# NASH VILLE EATS

**HOT CHICKEN, BUTTERMILK BISCUITS, AND 100 MORE SOUTHERN RECIPES** *FROM Music City*

**JENNIFER JUSTUS**          **PHOTOGRAPHY BY ANDREA BEHRENDS**

ABRAMS, NEW YORK

# Contents

# Contents

Nashville native, chef, and baker Phila Hach (right), photographed with the author.

**T**he first time I visited the Ryman Auditorium, the legendary church-turned-music-venue in downtown Nashville, I could hardly afford a show or even a ticket for the daytime tour. "How much is it?" I asked the tour attendant, a serious-looking woman with hair in tight white curls. "Thirteen dollars," she answered, peering at me over her spectacles as I calculated expenses. I eventually slid her a twenty under the glass. She printed my ticket and slid it back—along with my twenty-dollar bill. "Have a good time, honey," she said.

Nashville, I learned from that first visit many years ago, has a friendly, open way of welcoming folks and making them feel like they're home. Along Highway 100 during the 1950s, travelers could find Annie and Lon Loveless handing out biscuits and fried chicken through their front door. They turned their home into a restaurant and motel called the Loveless, and cooks still rise early at their old home place to make Annie's original biscuit recipe today.

Well before that in the 1800s, a widow named Lucinda "Granny" White baked ginger cake to give to travelers roadside until she opened a tavern and inn with hearty food and warm company. And that road, although paved now rather than dirt, still carries the name Granny White Pike.

In addition to those just passing through Nashville, the city draws the hopeful, the dreamers, and the entrepreneurs who come to stay. Many of those happen to be entertainers, troubadours, and raconteurs.

Nashvillians like to tell a good story, often in song. We're apt to throw a party for it and put on a show.

Our Nashville-style hot chicken, for instance, is as rowdy a party dish as they come. Fried and slathered with cayenne paste, it can make you sweat, swear, cry in your beer, and tremble with rock-and-roll salvation. I know that on the day of my divorce, it was the only thing I wanted to eat. Maybe I wanted to burn away the sadness. Or maybe I just wanted an entertaining diversion. Regardless, it's hard to think about much else while eating hot chicken.

The meat-and-three restaurants, our other culinary claim to fame, also have been hospitable to the travelers and locals alike, from the producer to the postman. By offering a daily choice of one meat along with three farm-fresh vegetables served cafeteria-style, they've kept many musicians from starving, as they pile their plates with slabs of tomato-glazed meat loaf and a ladleful of mashed potatoes and turnip greens like their mothers made. And to others, the meat-and-threes become boardrooms where deals go down. As late music journalist Chet Flippo wrote for *CMT News,* "Some music contracts have gravy stains on them."

That's part of why you'll find music in the form of playlists sprinkled throughout this book. Music and food both have a way of bringing us together and telling our stories. The playlists showcase artists from Nashville, and not just country musicians. While that genre helped establish Nashville as Music City, a vibrant scene with rock, jazz, and Grammy-winning symphony keeps our ears entertained and boots dancing.

Nashville now has one of the fastest-growing immigrant populations in the country with newcomers opening Burmese groceries, Kurdish markets, and taco trucks. A pioneer in that regard, Patti Myint opened the first Asian grocery here in 1975. After a robbery at the shop, she turned it into a restaurant to increase traffic for her safety. Neighbors welcomed it, and her son Arnold, whom she raised among the rows of tea tins and boxes of noodles, grew up to open restaurants of his own across the street before becoming a *Top Chef* contestant.

Another TV personality, Andrew Zimmern of *Bizarre Foods*, has noted that Nashvillians—with our musicians and creative vibes—"are good at being experimented at." We welcome new ideas and businesses, rather than waiting to see if they'll fail. Nashville wants to see what you've got.

So what exactly is "Nashville" food, anyway? Unlike the Low Country with its shrimp and grits, or even Memphis with its barbecue, Middle Tennessee doesn't have an easily recognized cuisine. We mostly celebrate simply what comes from the earth here—the corn, tomatoes, beans, greens—the animals that proved easiest to raise—such as hogs and chickens—with some wild game and fish from our waters. It's the food that business owners made into our meat-and-threes, tearooms, and chicken joints, and it's the baked hams and green beans traditionally served in our homes.

The recipes in this book reflect that in their ingredients and simple preparation, as do the stories about the farmers, cooks, makers, and musicians who call Nashville home. Though it nods to our roots, this is not a scholarly study or culinary history, but rather what I hope will be a connection between the past and the present. While a chicken recipe might be the easiest version to fry—hopefully encouraging new generations to indulge occasionally in that Sunday-afternoon activity handed down by our grandmothers—a recipe for squash casserole might look a bit more modern and light, layered with sour cream, pimientos, and topped with caramelized onions rather than the crunchy fried version from a can.

When I make these recipes, hands in cabbage for chowchow or pouring batter into a hot skillet with a hiss, I feel connected to this place and the people who came before me. It helps make sense of the agrarian lifestyles of those who first landed here and the ways Nashville's food has been shaped by people who have moved here, bringing their own preferences and creative ideas.

The dishes in these pages come from home kitchens, and they're fit for fish fries, church dinners, bridal luncheons, family reunion picnics, and backyard Sunday fundays. Perhaps the recipes will inspire in your home the hospitality and entertainment of this region.

It's my hope that you'll invite over friends and slide them a platter of chicken or bowl of green beans, welcoming them to your place and maybe thinking as you do, *Have a good time, honey.*

## KITCHEN PLAYLIST

The tunes of Nashville now span genres, reaching well beyond the city's country roots. This list demonstrates that diversity with a country legend, an East Nashville hippie folk singer, and two singer-songwriters.

**Nashville**
DAVID MEAD

After traveling many miles as an artist, David Mead sings about returning to town.

**Nashville Bum**
WAYLON JENNINGS

Though this book provides a better diet than what Waylon sings about in the song, his lyrics nod to the starving-artist stereotype with dinners of ketchup soup and Kool-Aid.

**Nashville**
TODD SNIDER

Known as the Tipsy Gypsy of East Nashville, Todd Snider found success outside the mainstream country machine with his folk music and witty observations.

**Home**
BEN RECTOR

This Tulsa native, now based in Nashville, helps represent the diversity of music being made here with his lively piano and horns. He sings about visiting other cities but finding home in Nashville.

Hospitality and tradition can be passed on through a plate of (Martin's Bar-B-Que Joint) ribs and Southern sides.

# THE RECIPES

—

# BISCUITs
# +
# PONES
# +
# ROLLS

Linda Carman often spends her days in a tiny test kitchen for Martha White, the aroma of her baking experiments perfuming the air. But as a child, she woke to the smell of biscuits every morning, too, and came home to cornbread every evening. Her mother carried on a farming tradition for a family that needed sustenance for long days. Then after studying home economics in college, Linda traveled Southern back roads to teach others how to cook and bake

at cooking schools, extension offices, and 4-H clubs, sometimes punching down the dough in the bowl that rode shotgun beside her. She understands what breads mean to people in this area.

The breads in this chapter include the types she—and many others from this region—hold dear, from pones of cornbread baked in heirloom skillets to the simplest corn dodgers flavored with bacon drippings. Biscuits will be served, too, along with simple but beloved accompaniments such as redeye gravy made with black coffee and ham drippings to a family recipe for sawmill gravy from songwriter Holly Williams.

In *Fortunes, Fiddles and Fried Chicken: A Business History of Nashville*, author Bill Carey notes that at the turn of the nineteenth to the twentieth century, flour was Nashville's number one export. Companies even outside the area found it profitable to ship grain to Nashville from the Midwest on the L&N railroad line. Grain would be ground and packaged there, then distributed.

After the invention of commercial leavening agents, self-rising flour took hold in Southern kitchens beginning in the late 1800s, when a Nashville concern called the Owsley Flour Company began to mass-produce it. Other brands with more staying power followed, including Royal Flour Mill in 1899, with its Martha White line named for the founder's daughter.

By 1948, Martha White had tapped into the growing country music business in Nashville by sponsoring the Grand Ole Opry despite an advertising budget of just twenty-five dollars a week. The company hired an unknown bluegrass group called the Foggy Mountain Boys (led by Lester Flatt and Earl Scruggs) to tour the South and play shows to tout the brand. They became known as the "World's Greatest Flour Peddlers" and toured widely on the Martha White Bluegrass Express bus. Many others musicians like Alison Krauss have followed in their footsteps through the years.

But beyond the flour companies, cooks turned the raw ingredients into those golden-tinted orbs of biscuit or cornmeal for spreading with butter or a slow roll of sorghum. Lon and Annie Loveless served biscuits from their private home to travelers along US Highway 100 and made a business of it as the Loveless Motel and Cafe. The creaky hardwood floors have borne the weight of many steps, from twirling dancers at the Lovelesses' house parties in the 1940s to servers delivering trays of fried chicken and biscuits to customers.

While the motel part of the property has been converted back into shops and ownership has changed hands, Annie's original biscuit recipe still draws a varied group of locals, tourists, and cyclists fueling up for a ride down the nearby Natchez Trace Parkway. The Oliphant family, for example, has gathered at the Loveless every Easter for half a century. And at least one customer returns on his wedding anniversary each year to sit at his and his wife's favorite table, even though she's no longer here.

Relative newcomers like Karl and Sarah Worley of Biscuit Love Brunch carry on the biscuit tradition by reviving the cracker-like beaten biscuits at their shop, and they keep it modern, too, with their biscuit sandwiches of fried hot chicken, a drizzle of honey, and house-made pickles. The couple paid their dues schlepping lunch in a food truck to office parks and selling to rowdy crowds at music festivals until 2015, when they opened a brick-and-mortar shop in the Gulch area of Nashville. A formerly gritty-looking part of town where the trains from the L&N line once met, it's now a spot where glassy condos and hot restaurants have sprouted, so it's a fitting spot to keep one foot in tradition and another pointing toward a more modern South.

Even before biscuits, many of the most beloved breads in the South were baked by Native Americans using cornmeal. Traditional recipes include the simple cornmeal-and-water dough that bakes into dodgers or the round pones that have been sharpened and moistened with buttermilk. We slice and share them at the table like savory pies for sopping up pot likker or split them open to steam and smother with white beans and chowchow.

A few handed-down rules apply to some of these breads. Keep the biscuits small enough to warrant taking two and leave the bigger versions for the restaurants. As for Southern cornbread, we use white cornmeal more often than yellow, and though we're apt to slip a spoonful of sugar into just about anything Southern, we'd rather you don't when it comes to the cornbread.

But overall, these breads are easy, with basic ingredients and simple steps for whipping up batches as regularly as you'd like. And they're the texture of what grows here—you can feel it as you make, serve, and break these breads together at the table.

## KITCHEN PLAYLIST

Alice Jarman, the first test kitchen director for Martha White, often traveled with bands on the company's bluegrass bus. Between sets she would put on live advertisements by demonstrating how to make fried chicken and biscuits. So when the bus broke down during one tour, she told her protégée Linda Carman, "We just sat on the side of the road and ate the commercial."

**Foggy Mountain Breakdown**
LESTER FLATT AND EARL SCRUGGS

This song, along with the jingle "You Bake Right with Martha White," became two of the band's most requested. Even during a performance and taping at Carnegie Hall in New York City, a guest kept shouting for "Martha White!" until the band had no choice but to oblige.

**How Many Biscuits Can You Eat?**
DR. HUMPHREY BATE AND HIS POSSUM HUNTERS

Dr. Humphrey, a Vanderbilt graduate and physician, also happened to be one of the great country harmonica players and the first performer ever broadcast on the Grand Ole Opry.

**Biscuits**
KACEY MUSGRAVES

This Nashville-based artist from Texas took home two Grammys with her album *Same Trailer, Different Park*. Known for her witty lyrics, she sings in this song about minding your own business.

**Keep My Skillet Good and Greasy**
UNCLE DAVE MACON

One of the first favorites of the Grand Ole Opry, this old-time banjo player first performed in vaudeville.

# *Phila Hach*

The local legend serves up a mix of life wisdom with resourceful farm upbringing.

When Phila Hach makes biscuits, she doesn't mess with measuring cups, pastry cutters, or spoons. She plunges her fingers directly into the mound of flour and cream. "What is life except for the feel?" she asked, batting the dough with swift experience as the bowl rattled against the counter.

She made her first batch of biscuits at age two in 1928. It's how her mother taught her to count: "One . . . two . . . ," she remembers, folding the dough over on the floured surface and stopping just past ten. Then the eighty-eight-year-old chef cut the dough into circles with an old snuff can from a brand that's long been discontinued. "I used to have hundreds of these and gave them away," she says.

Growing up on a farm with a Swiss mother, who also worked as one of the first home demonstrators in Middle Tennessee, Phila picked up cooking early and easily. She still recalls peering over the edge of a saucepan to watch the magic transformation of an egg cracked onto the hot surface. Yet with the lessons of the country around her, she longed to study the city, too. "I want to learn," she told a hiring manager at the airline where she took a job as stewardess in the 1930s. "I still do," she says now. "But it takes guts to step out there and be your authentic self."

It also took guts to walk into the kitchens of the world's best hotels and ask to cook alongside the chefs. That's what she did at the Savoy in London and the George V in Paris during layovers. She gathered tastes and techniques like stamps in a passport, adding a worldly touch to her strong Southern foundation.

She wrote the first catering manual for the airlines in the 1930s and then became a local celebrity as hostess of the first cooking show in the South, welcoming June Carter Cash and Duncan Hines the man, among others, to her table.

She married a German tobacco importer whom she had met briefly in the lobby of a swanky Parisian hotel. He offered to carry her bags, and she politely refused his help. A few years later, he moved to Tennessee, turned on his television, and the lovely American flight attendant was looking back at him in black-and-white. He wrote to her, but she tossed his note into the garbage—for a moment. Then, on second thought, she fished it out of the wastebasket and accepted his offer for a date. "I never saw another man," she says. They honeymooned for a year before opening Hachland Hill Dining Inn just outside Nashville.

Even with her travels, Phila has remained rooted in her Tennessee farmland upbringing, which instilled in her an honest resourcefulnes—the ability to make the best of what's on hand. "What is intriguing to me still are the resources our land supplies us with. But the most intriguing to me is the resources of our ingenuity," she says. "When I was growing up, we had no grocery store. What did we need? Sometimes in our life, we get all mixed up. What we want is not necessarily what we need."

With her white hair pulled into a tight bun, she ties on an ankle-length apron (it's where she keeps her cell phone) before buzzing through her kitchen. She imparts her wisdom partly through the seventeen cookbooks she penned, sometimes for making biscuits and other times on living life.

"One of the things that I learned is to be free in the way that you live. Don't make work out of anything. When people say 'I'm gonna work on it,' I say 'work on what?' I'm all about the moment," she says, "because, it's gone."

# Country Pain Perdu

When friends visit, as they often do, Phila Hach still displays the ingenuity and resourcefulness she's called on for years, like many who grew up in this region. She might pull together this *pain perdu* made with half a loaf of nearly stale bread and egg yolks. Topped with tomato and slices of bacon and paired with a grated carrot salad, it's simple, chic, and as comfortable on the plate in Tennessee as it is in Europe. "What more could you want?" she asks.

**Makes 4 servings**

4   large egg yolks

1⅓  cups (315 ml) whole milk

½   teaspoon sea salt

½   teaspoon black pepper

½   cup (60 g) yellow cornmeal

1   teaspoon dried oregano

2   small tomatoes

4   thickly cut slices bread (I used a Tuscan-style boule)

1½  teaspoons to 1 tablespoon extra-virgin olive oil

1   tablespoon butter

8   slices bacon

1   tablespoon finely grated Parmesan cheese

In a small bowl, combine the egg yolks, milk, salt, and pepper.

In a separate bowl, combine the cornmeal and oregano. Slice the tomatoes and place them on paper towels.

Place the bread flat in a casserole dish. Pour the egg mixture over it and let it sit while you heat a sauté pan over medium-high. Add just enough of the oil to coat the pan, and then add the butter. When the oil and butter are hot, carefully move the bread with a spatula from the casserole pan to the sauté pan.

Fry the bread for about 2 minutes on each side, until it is golden and brown and crispy in places. Set the bread aside. Remove the pan from the heat and wipe out excess oil with a paper towel. Return the pan to the heat and add the bacon. Fry until they reach the desired crispness.

Meanwhile, dredge the tomatoes in the cornmeal mixture. When the bacon is done, remove it from the pan and pour off a bit of the grease, leaving just about 1 tablespoon, and then fry the tomatoes for about 2 minutes on each side, until the cornmeal mixture is lightly browned.

Top the bread with the tomatoes and sprinkle with Parmesan cheese. Drape the bacon across the tomatoes and serve.

# Phila's Make-Do Biscuits

Phila's biscuits have been featured in documentaries, newspaper articles, and magazine spreads. She can make them with buttermilk or cream, with yeast or without leavening. But on the day we visited, she wanted to show us yet another way of making do with what she had in the cupboard and fridge.

These biscuits feel light despite the sour cream and have a breath of orange, as you'd expect from the ingredient list. Regardless of your experience with biscuits, these are truly simple to whip up.

**Makes about a dozen biscuits (depending on the size of your cutter)**

1 **cup (125 g) self-rising flour, plus more for turning out dough**

½ **cup (120 ml) full-fat sour cream**

**Splash of orange juice (about 2 tablespoons)**

Preheat the oven to 450°F (230°C). Use convection if you have it.

Combine the flour, sour cream, and orange juice with your hands, working quickly and stopping as soon as a dough forms—be careful not to overdo it. If you feel like you need it, sprinkle on a little more orange juice.

Turn the dough out onto a floured surface and fold it over twelve times. Cut the biscuits into rounds by pressing the cutter straight down and place them close together on a baking sheet. Combine the scraps if you would like by pressing them together just once or twice to use up all the dough.

Bake for 10 to 15 minutes. If you're not using convection, which I do not have, you might find these biscuits to be flatter and less golden on top. That's okay. They'll be more brown on the bottom and cooked through. Serve them warm with butter, sorghum, honey, or your favorite preserves.

# Kathryn's Mini Apple Cheddar Biscuits

Kathryn Johnson, a Nashville food blogger at ladysmokey.com, cohosts occasional Sunday afternoon potlucks with live music. For these soirées, she often makes these biscuits. They're a hit for their bits of apple and cheese, and for being crispy on the outside and moist inside.

**Makes 2 dozen mini biscuits cut into about 2-inch (5-cm) rounds**

2  cups (250 g) all-purpose soft wheat flour (Kathryn uses White Lily unbleached bread flour)

1  cup (120 g) whole wheat pastry flour

2  tablespoons baking powder

1  teaspoon sea salt

6  tablespoons (85 g) unsalted butter, cut into ½-inch (12-mm) pieces, chilled

1  cup (181 g) peeled and grated apple

1  cup (120 g) shredded extra-sharp white cheddar

1  cup (240 ml) buttermilk

Preheat the oven to 450°F (230°C).

In a medium bowl, mix together both flours, the baking powder, and salt. Add the butter, working it into the flour with your fingertips until the pieces are a little larger than an English pea but not larger than a lima bean. Work quickly, but gently, so that the heat of your hands doesn't melt the butter.

Add the grated apple and cheese. Then pour in all of the buttermilk and, using light pressure, fold the mixture a few times until it holds together. Don't overmix. In order to make light biscuits, it is important to work the dough as little as possible.

Turn the dough out onto a floured board and fold it quickly and gently four to six times, just enough to get all the ingredients mixed.

Sprinkle a little flour under the dough and lightly dust the top of the dough so that it won't stick. Roll the dough out to about ½ inch (12 mm) thickness. Cut the dough into 2-inch (5-cm) rounds. Place them on an ungreased baking sheet so that they are touching, and bake the biscuits for about 12 minutes. They will be light in color on top with the bits of cheese turning brown. Serve warm or at room temperature.

# Beaten Biscuits

Beaten biscuits came along before the invention of commercial leavening, back when the dough literally took a beating: several hundred strikes with a mallet until it blistered, causing pockets of air. Inventors later created a hand-cranked machine called a biscuit break to make the process somewhat easier, but it still required time, attention, and energy rarely put forth in home kitchens today. All the rolling, cranking, and beating produces a light, flat circle that's more crackerlike than the puffed-up biscuits we know today. Beaten biscuits were the type of snack you could slip into your pocket before work and leave for a few days without worrying about them going stale.

Home cooks can, however, try this recipe using a food processor. It's similar to a version that ran in an article by Nashville writer John Egerton in the *New York Times* in December 1983. And with their small, round shape, eating one can feel like taking communion with reverence for time and tradition.

**Makes about 2 dozen biscuits that are 1 ½ inches (38 mm) in diameter**

2½ cups (315 g) all-purpose flour

½ heaping teaspoon baking powder

½ teaspoon salt

1 tablespoon sugar

½ cup (100 g) lard or vegetable shortening (lard is preferred)

¾ cup (180 ml) heavy cream, very cold (nearly icy)

Position one oven rack at the bottom and one at the top, then preheat the oven to 325°F (165°C).

Sift together the flour, baking powder, salt, and sugar.

Using a pastry cutter, cut in the lard until the mixture looks like coarse meal. Add the cream and knead the dough into a ball. Divide the mixture in half and whirl each piece for 2 minutes in a food processor fitted with the dough blade.

Recombine the two pieces of dough, roll it out, and fold it several times. When the dough is smooth, cut the biscuits into 1 ½-inch (38-mm) circles. Pierce each biscuit two or three times with a fork to allow air to escape from the layers during baking.

Bake the biscuits on the bottom rack for 5 minutes and then move them to the top rack for about 25 to 30 minutes. They should be very lightly golden and firm. Serve them with very thinly sliced pieces (almost like shavings) of country ham.

# Sawmill Sausage Gravy

Holly Williams, daughter to Hank Williams Jr., granddaughter to Hank Williams Sr., and a talented singer-songwriter in her own right, makes this sausage gravy when she bakes biscuits for her family. She learned to prepare this gravy from her mother, who learned from her grandmother, making this a family tradition too.

**Makes about 2 cups (480 ml)**

1  pound (455 g) mild breakfast sausage meat

½  cup (60 g) all-purpose flour

About 2 ½ cups (600 ml) whole milk

¼  teaspoon salt

¼  teaspoon black pepper

Heat a medium saucepan over medium heat and add the sausage. Cook until brown, about 6 minutes, breaking it up with the back of the spoon. Remove the sausage from the pan.

Begin incorporating the flour and milk, adding about 2 tablespoons of each at a time, whisking constantly. Continue adding the flour and milk until the gravy is thickened but still thin enough to pour. Stir the sausage back into the gravy, season with the salt and pepper, and serve warm over biscuits.

# Redeye Gravy

A generous splash of morning coffee plus the bits left in the pan from frying slices of ham produces a simple, ingenious moistener for the morning bread. Butter added to the drippings softens and readies the mixture for a biscuit, while brown sugar balances out the salt in the ham. This gravy might get its name from the red hue it casts or maybe because we're red-eyed in the morning.

**Makes about 1 cup (240 ml)**

Drippings from 1 pound (455 g) country ham (see page 115 for country ham preparation)

1  tablespoon butter

½  cup (120 ml) brewed coffee

2  tablespoons dark brown sugar

In the same cast-iron skillet in which you prepared the ham, add the butter to the drippings and cook over medium-high until the butter has melted. Add the coffee, brown sugar, and 1 cup (240 ml) water, stirring to combine. Bring the mixture to a boil. Reduce the heat and simmer for about 1 minute. Pour into a gravy boat or individual ramekins for serving.

Karl Worley serves beaten biscuits
at his shop, Biscuit Love Brunch.

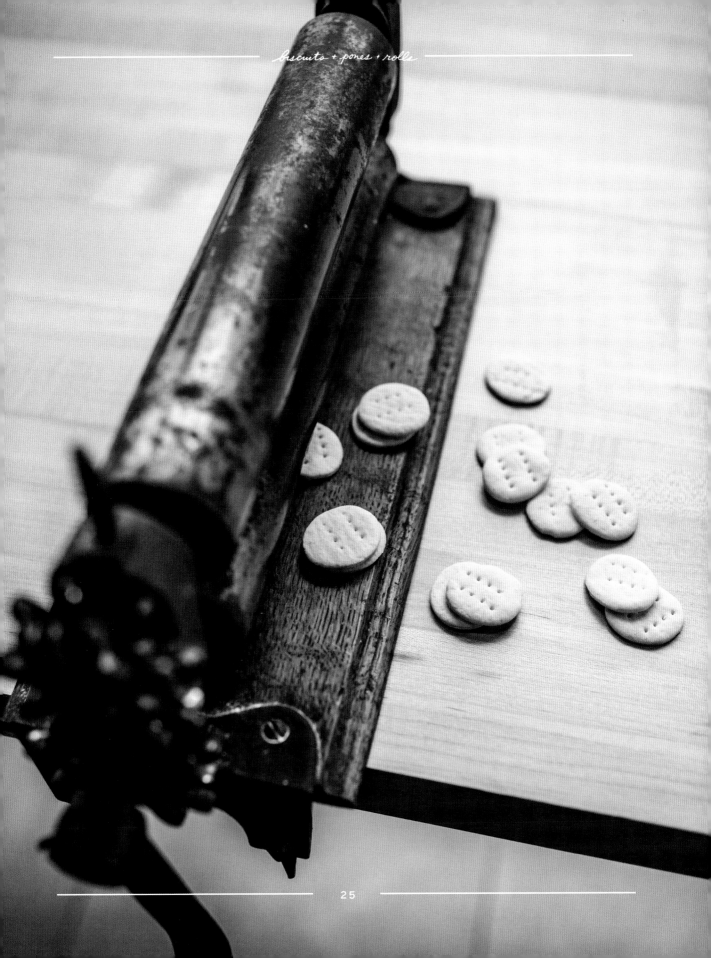

# Buttermilk Biscuits

Everyone needs a straightforward biscuit recipe to practice and master. Though this recipe calls for butter, feel free to experiment with the type of fat you prefer. Linda Carman of Martha White prefers shortening to the butter, for example, as she likes to taste the flavor of the wheat, which grows softer in this part of the country. Meanwhile, some of Nashville's most famous biscuit houses prefer the flavor of lard.

**Makes 14 to 24 biscuits, depending on the size of the cutter**

½ cup (1 stick/115 g) butter, chilled

2 cups (250 g) all-purpose flour, plus more for sprinkling

2 teaspoons baking powder

¼ teaspoon baking soda

1 tablespoon sugar

1 teaspoon salt

1 cup (240 ml) buttermilk

Preheat the oven to 450°F (230°C).

Cut the butter into pieces about the size of a chickpea and place them in the freezer while you prepare the other ingredients.

Into a medium bowl, sift together the flour, baking powder, baking soda, sugar, and salt. Using your hands and moving as quickly and lightly as possible, work the butter into the flour until the mixture is just combined. It will be mealy-looking, with some butter pieces about the size of a pea. Mix in the buttermilk, being careful not to overmix. The dough should still be slightly sticky, and the flour should be incorporated but not perfectly mixed.

Turn the dough out onto a floured surface and sprinkle a little more flour on top to keep it from sticking as you fold it over six times. Press it down to about a ½-inch (12-mm) thickness. Cut it into rounds and place the biscuits close together on a baking sheet. Combine the scraps if you would like by pressing them together just once or twice to use up all the dough. Bake until they are golden, about 10 to 12 minutes depending on the size of the biscuits. Serve warm.

# Cornbread Dodgers

Writer and Southern Foodways Alliance cofounder John Egerton once made corn pones similar to these to kick off a *Tennessean* newspaper series I wrote about home cooking.

I prefer these dodgers to another Southern favorite, hot water cornbread, which is prepared with similar ingredients but fried rather than baked. The dodgers produce an earthy aroma like corn tortillas as you add the hot water to the cornmeal, then sweeten as they bake. Crunchy on the outside and soft inside, they're perfect for dunking and scooping.

**Makes about 8 dodgers**

2 cups (245 g) white cornmeal

½ teaspoon kosher or sea salt

1 tablespoon hot bacon drippings

3 cups (720 ml) boiling water

Preheat the oven to 425°F (220°C).

Combine the cornmeal and salt in a bowl. Add the bacon drippings and then the boiling water, stirring it in slowly, until a thick mush forms; it should be the consistency of mashed potatoes, but not too thick. Spoon the batter onto an ungreased cookie sheet, being careful to keep the mounds no thicker than a deck of cards. Piling the cornmeal mixture too high makes them too thick and thus mushy in the middle.

Bake the dodgers for about 35 minutes, then flip them over and continue baking for another 10 minutes. They should be very light brown in color.

# Traditional Skillet Cornbread

The funny thing about family recipes is they can be handed down with both too much information *and* not enough. My grandfather J.J.'s cornbread, passed on from my mother, includes self-rising flour and an additional pinch of baking powder. When I asked Mom why she includes it, she said, "Because J.J. told me to."

Though he's no longer around to answer the question firsthand, I asked a professional, Linda Carman of the Martha White Test Kitchen, who said adding a smidgen of extra leavening to self-rising flour sometimes helps offset the acid in buttermilk, which can compromise the leavening.

So the recipe is missing that info—but it did include a long set of instructions on putting out a grease fire (which I have omitted here), as well as a reminder to "call your mother."

**Makes 8 generous servings**

1 cup (125 g) self-rising flour

1 cup (140 g) self-rising white cornmeal

Pinch of baking soda

Pinch of baking powder

¼ teaspoon kosher or sea salt

1 large egg, beaten

1½ cups (360 ml) buttermilk

¼ cup (60 ml) bacon drippings

Position one oven rack at the bottom and one at the top, then preheat the oven to 450°F (230°C).

In a medium bowl, combine the flour, cornmeal, baking soda, baking powder, and salt. Form an indentation in the middle of the flour mixture and pour in first the egg and then 1¼ cups (300 ml) of the buttermilk. Stir the ingredients to combine and gradually add the remaining ¼ cup (60 ml) buttermilk until the mixture is smooth and soupy.

Pour the bacon drippings into a cast-iron skillet and place it over medium heat until it is shimmering. Pour two-thirds of the hot grease into the cornbread mixture and quickly combine. Add the cornmeal mixture to the hot skillet and place it in the oven. Reduce the temperature to 425°F (220°C) and bake for 20 to 25 minutes. The edges should be caramel-colored and the top golden brown. If the edges begin to brown too quickly during baking, move the skillet to the top rack and continue cooking. Cool the cornbread for 5 to 10 minutes before turning it out of the skillet onto a plate. Slice and serve warm.

# Corn Light Bread

This old-fashioned recipe for a loaf cornbread that's also part cake comes from Nashville chef Guerry McComas. He passed it along from his Aunt Francis Jackson. It's just about the only time a true Southerner welcomes sugar in the cornbread. Keep in mind that the cornmeal mush needs to sit overnight before you can mix up and bake the batter.

**Makes two 9-inch (23-cm) loaves**

| | |
|---|---|
| 6 | cups (1.4 L) cold water |
| ¼ | teaspoon kosher salt |
| 5 ⅓ | cups (650 g) white cornmeal |
| 1 | cup (200 g) sugar |
| 1 | teaspoon baking soda |
| 2 | teaspoons kosher salt |
| 2 | heaping teaspoons vegetable shortening, melted, plus more for greasing pan |

Bring 3 cups (720 ml) of the water to a boil. Stir in the salt, then add 1⅓ cups (160 g) of the cornmeal and cook the mixture into a mush, about 2 minutes. Remove the pan from the heat and stir in the remaining 3 cups (720 ml) cold water. Add the remaining 4 cups (490 g) cornmeal; this will make the batter thick, like for corn pones. Let it stand overnight, covered and at room temperature.

The next day, set the oven to 425°F (220°C) and place two greased loaf pans in it to heat. Add the sugar, baking soda, salt, and shortening to the cornmeal mixture. Divide the batter between the two hot loaf pans and bake for about 50 minutes, until the cornbread is deep golden and browning around the edges. Serve it sliced.

# Yeast Dinner Muffins

Yeast rolls make the table in homes, tearooms, and diners around the South, but this bread tastes like a cross between a biscuit and a roll. This recipe, passed along to me by Middle Tennesseean 4-H teacher Barbara Davenport, is by far the easiest and most no-fail dinner bread I've encountered.

**Makes about a dozen muffins**

| | |
|---|---|
| 1 | package (2 ¼ teaspoons/10 g) dry yeast |
| ½ | cup (1 stick/115 g) butter, melted and cooled, plus more for greasing pan |
| 3 | cups (375 g) self-rising flour |
| ⅓ | cup (65 g) sugar |

Preheat the oven to 400°F (205°C). Grease a standard muffin pan.

In a medium bowl, combine 1½ cups (360 ml) water with the yeast and butter. Add the flour and sugar to the liquid and mix well. Pour the batter into the prepared pan and bake for about 20 minutes or until the rolls are golden and beginning to brown at the edges. They are best served warm.

# Jalapeño Cornbread

Dorothy Riddell, known as Dot to her friends and Grandmama to Robin Riddell Jones, makes this moist, peppered cornbread for family gatherings or in bulk for trips to the nursing home or friends' houses. So when Robin moved to Nashville more than a decade ago, she brought the recipe with her. She makes it about once a week to serve along with soup or for slicing thinly and warming in the toaster as a snack. And just like her grandmama, Robin takes this bread to friends' homes when they have babies or feel ill or just need their day brightened.

Peppers are a popular addition to cornbread for many bakers. Journalist and musician Peter Cooper also recalled a favorite jalapeño-spiked cornbread from Earl Scruggs's birthday parties that was made by the late Dixie Hall, wife of the acclaimed songwriter Tom T. Hall.

**Makes 8 generous servings**

¼ cup (60 ml) vegetable oil

2 large eggs, slightly beaten

1 cup (240 ml) sour cream

1 cup (254 g) cream-style corn

1½ cups (205 g) self-rising cornmeal

1 teaspoon kosher or sea salt

2 tablespoons chopped green bell pepper

2 tablespoons chopped jalapeño pepper, seeds and ribs removed

1 cup (120 g) shredded sharp cheddar cheese

Set the oven to 450°F (230°C). Pour the oil into a cast-iron skillet and allow it to heat in the oven while you prepare the cornbread. (Keep a close eye on it. Be careful not to let it get too hot or leave it unattended.)

In a medium bowl, combine the eggs, sour cream, corn, cornmeal, salt, peppers, and cheese. Pour about half of the hot oil from the skillet into the batter, leaving the rest in the pan. Stir the oil into the batter and then pour the batter into the hot skillet. Ideally, you'll hear a sizzle.

Bake the cornbread for 20 to 25 minutes, until golden on top and browning at the edges with cornbread pulling away from the skillet. Serve it warm or at room temperature.

## THE RECIPES

—

# STARTERS + SALADS

# A
quick way to make people feel comfortable in your home is to offer them something to eat. And maybe hand them a drink. But we'll get to that part later.

A little nibble before the main event sets the tone and can hint toward what's ahead. But maybe more important, it says right from the start, "I'm going to take care of you, and I'm glad you're here."

The recipes in this section offer a few different ways to extend your hospitality, including trusted favorites like delicate cheese straws that melt in the mouth; deviled eggs with a decidedly Nashville kick; and pimiento cheese, along with the tales of its Nashville connections.

We've included a couple soups that showcase Nashville's past and present, such as onion bisque inspired by the historic Hermitage Hotel, which has served a version for more than a century. Then, from a newer Nashville, Kurdish refugees who have put down roots here share the hearty and simple lentil soup that breaks the Ramadan fast. Though they're served in different settings, both of these soups shine and call for just a few ingredients.

As for the salads in this section, you'll find the classic potato salad and cooling coleslaws, as well as a modernized version of the tomato cucumber salad, grounded with earthy tahini and splinters of carrot to add color and crunch. Perfect for the backyard barbecue and the reunion or church picnic, when you take the hospitality to go.

## KITCHEN PLAYLIST

This list celebrates a few of Music City's country queens.

**Tennessee Homesick Blues**
DOLLY PARTON

This ditty was featured in the movie *Rhinestone*, and Dolly wrote this song about her home state.

**Miss Being Mrs.**
LORETTA LYNN

Nashville-based musician and producer Jack White worked with Loretta Lynn on this record.

**Crazy**
PATSY CLINE

Though her hits, like this one written by Willie Nelson, eventually crossed over to pop, Cline was the first female solo artist to be inducted into the Country Music Hall of Fame.

**It Wasn't God Who Made Honky Tonk Angels**
KITTY WELLS

This hit helped make Kitty Wells the first female country music star who paved the way for many others.

# Noble Springs Dairy + The Bloomy Rind

Justyne Noble cares for a goat that will someday bring Tennesseans her cheeses.

The latest arrival at Noble Springs Dairy Farm, a two-day-old kid, stumbled and skipped near its mother as it caught the attention of the older goats. With their wise-looking beards, they peered over the barn fence, nosy and maybe a little judgmental, like the elder Muppets in the opera seats. Even the farm dog breezed through to sniff out the situation. "They're all really curious about the babies," says farm co-owner Justyne Noble.

Along with her husband, Dustin, Justyne cares for the goats that provide milk for their cheeses—logs of fresh chevre, tangy feta in brine, wheels of gouda, and soft ripened goat cheeses. And beyond understanding the cheese-making dance of science and art, Justyne can tick off the baby's lineage like a proud aunt.

Justyne and Dustin are two of just a handful of farmstead cheese makers in Tennessee. Nashville cheese monger Kathleen Cotter, the mastermind behind the Southern Artisan Cheese Festival, has helped promote their business and the businesses of other cheese makers since she launched her company, The Bloomy Rind, in 2010. And she explains the lack of cheese makers in the area simply: "Cheese making is a hard thing."

MILL CREEK GOUDA
King's Kreamery, PA
Semi-firm and fudgy. Slightly sharp & tangy
Past. cow $23/LB
Cave Aged Tomme
Marcoot Jersey Creamery, IL
Harder aged tomme. Buttery, salty & peppery.
Raw. Cow $19.5/LB
Cumberland

**Kathleen Cotter helps promote local cheesemakers through her company, The Bloomy Rind.**

The Southern Artisan Cheese Festival draws hundreds of attendees and about 20 cheese makers for sampling and education, including the Nobles, who have grown their operation from about 35 goats in 2009 to 136. They milk about 75 to 80 gallons a day during peak season to make about 10,000 pounds of cheese a year.

But despite all the work, Dustin calls it a labor of love and a dream realized from his early interest in goats and food production.

Coming from a long line of Nashvillians in the food business, Dustin's great-grandfather moved to the area in the early 1900s and opened a drugstore as well as Noble's Restaurant at the corner of Old Hickory and Franklin Road. His grandfather took over the business and ran it as a meat-and-three restaurant and six-room hotel.

Meanwhile, Dustin's parents discovered when he was an infant that he had an allergy to cow's milk. Some friends suggested goat's milk, and he's been interested in the animals ever since. When a family friend's father put his farmland into conservation easement and asked Dustin and Justyne if they would like to raise goats and make cheese on the land, they jumped at the chance.

These days Justyne might look after the baby goats and herd while Dustin will head back into the shop to finish up a batch of cheese.

The interplay works for the couple, even with the wrangling, milking, and making of cheese, with its temperature gauges, enzymes, curds, and whey.

Kathleen once again summed it up in simple terms we can appreciate as we spread fresh chevre on a warm slice of toast and drizzle it with honey.

"It's sunshine to grass to milk to cheese," she says. "So it's like you're eating sunshine."

# Bloomy Rind Beer Cheese

Kathleen Cotter sells a version of this beer cheese at the shop she shares with Porter Road Butcher in East Nashville. This dip comes together quickly and easily with the whirl of a food processor, but the combination of cheeses with garlic, cayenne, and a good glug of local beer give it a full, sharp flavor.

**Makes about 8 servings**

½  pound (277 g) aged sharp cheddar, roughly chopped (Kathleen uses four-year-old Hook's from Wisconsin)

¼  pound (114 g) soft cow's milk cheese (Kathleen uses Lil' Moo from Sweet Grass Dairy)

1  clove garlic, finely grated (ideally with a Microplane)

1  teaspoon dry mustard

¼  teaspoon black pepper

¼  teaspoon cayenne pepper

1  teaspoon Worcestershire sauce

½  teaspoon cayenne hot sauce

12  ounces (360 ml) beer (Kathleen uses locally brewed Yazoo Gerst)

Pretzels or crackers for serving

In a food processor, combine the cheeses, garlic, mustard, and black and cayenne peppers, Worcestershire and cayenne sauces, and beer and whip until the mixture is smooth. Chill the spread for at least 30 minutes. Then allow it to come back up to room temperature before serving it with pretzels or crackers.

# Classic Pimiento Cheese

Southerners might not have invented pimiento cheese, but we've sure done our best to claim it.

The spread has kept its place on tables here in both high and low culture—from tearoom sandwiches presented on tiered silver trays to the diagonally cut variety served on a paper plate at the drugstore counter. It also played a role in empowering women entrepreneurs even before they could vote. Eugenia Duke, for example, founder of Duke's Mayonnaise in Greenville, South Carolina, sold pimiento cheese sandwiches from her home to textile mill workers as well as downtown hotels. Later in the 1950s, a Nashville secretary named Grace Grissom mortgaged all she owned to create Mrs. Grissom's pimiento cheese, still found in groceries today.

This version stays classic and straightforward with plenty of pimientos in every bite, because that's the ingredient that makes this spread unique. Worcestershire, hot sauce, and parsley add color and pop.

**Makes about 1½ cups (360 ml)**

4   ounces (115 g) extra-sharp white cheddar cheese, shredded

4   ounces (115 g) mild yellow cheddar, shredded

1   (4-ounce/113-g) jar diced pimientos, drained

¼   cup (60 ml) mayonnaise (I like Duke's brand)

1   tablespoon finely chopped fresh parsley

½   tablespoon Worcestershire sauce

About 6 drops cayenne hot sauce

A good pinch of black pepper

In a medium bowl, toss together the cheeses. Add the remaining ingredients to the bowl and stir to combine. Refrigerate the spread for an hour or more before serving.

Dustin Noble removes wheels of
pressed cheese from their moulds.

The Nobles make their Southall gouda
with a firm goat's milk cheese in the style
of the Dutch classic.

# Pimiento Goat Cheese

This Southern party starter delivers a rowdy little punch in a sophisticated-looking package. The sour cream helps mellow the flavor of the goat cheese while the scallions, garlic, and pepper bring kick in their own ways.

In lieu of crackers, serve it with celery sticks, carrot sticks, and radishes, or stuffed into grape tomatoes for a crudité platter.

**Makes about 1½ cups (360ml) or enough to fit snugly into a 4-inch-by-2-inch (10-cm-by-5-cm) serving dish**

5   ounces (140 g) soft goat cheese

½   cup (120 ml) sour cream

1   (4-ounce/113-g) jar diced pimientos, drained

2   medium scallions, thinly sliced

1   clove garlic, finely chopped

¼   teaspoon black pepper

Fresh parsley for garnish

Celery sticks, carrot sticks, and radishes for serving

In a small bowl, combine the goat cheese, sour cream, pimientos, scallions, garlic, and pepper. Chill the spread for at least 30 minutes to allow the flavors to come together.

Just before serving, spoon the pimiento cheese into a ramekin and garnish it with a sprig of fresh parsley. Serve with celery, carrot and radishes for dipping.

# Cheese Straws

Robin Riddell Jones learned to make these cheese straws (actually, they're shaped more like shortbread cookies than straws) from her grandmother in Mississippi, and she carried the recipe with her to Nashville, where she serves them at her holiday parties. These appetizers pair well with cocktails and wine and practically melt in the mouth, leaving just a tiny kick of cayenne.

**Makes about 2 dozen**

8   ounces (225 g) extra-sharp cheese, finely shredded, room temperature

1   stick (113 g) salted butter, room temperature

1   teaspoon cayenne pepper

½   teaspoon fine sea salt

1½   cups plus 2 tablespoons (205 g) all-purpose flour, sifted

Preheat the oven to 325°F (165°C). Line a cookie sheet with parchment paper.

In a medium bowl, using an electric mixer, combine the cheese and butter. Add the cayenne and salt while mixing. Add the flour gradually until combined.

Pack the dough into a cookie press and shape it into flat rectangles about 2 inches (5 cm) long and 1 inch (2.5 cm) wide, placed about two fingers apart on the prepared cookie sheet. Bake the cheese straws for about 15 minutes but watch them carefully to ensure that they don't burn. Serve them warm or at room temperature.

# Country Ham Salad

Bob Woods shared this recipe for ham salad, which he learned from his grandmother. He makes a version of it at his shop, The Hamery, where his family has cured hams since the 1960s.

**Makes about 5 sandwiches or 10 servings as a dip**

½  pound (225 g) country ham, chopped

½  tablespoon sugar

1  tablespoon spicy brown mustard

⅓  cup (80 ml) mayonnaise

4  tablespoons India relish (or sweet pickle relish or sweet chowchow from page 193)

¼  cup (30 g) chopped onion

¼  cup (100 g) chopped celery

3  hard-cooked eggs, peeled and finely diced

Combine all the ingredients in a food processor and pulse until ingredients are combined and ham is finely chopped. Refrigerate the salad for about an hour to let the flavors come together. Remove it from the refrigerator about 30 minutes before serving with crackers or spread on white bread.

# Hot Sausage Balls

Though they may not be the most sophisticated or complicated of canapés, sausage balls have long been a staple of the holiday appetizer table and football tailgate spreads across the South. I like to dress them up and add texture by stacking them atop fried apple wedges.

As for the apple component, Southerners have been known to "fry" apples in bacon grease. I choose butter, but that doesn't make them any less tasty when paired with breakfast pork. And since cheddar cheese also pairs well with apples, this makes for a spicy, cheesy combo.

**Makes about 50 pieces**

1 cup (125 g) all-purpose flour

1½ teaspoons baking powder

¼ teaspoon black pepper

2¾ cups (330 g) shredded sharp cheddar cheese

1 pound (455 g) spicy breakfast sausage

1 tablespoon butter, melted

Fried apples for serving (recipe follows)

Preheat the oven to 350°F (190°C).

Using your hands, combine the flour, baking powder, pepper, cheese, sausage, and butter in a medium bowl. Roll the mixture into walnut-size balls and place them on an ungreased baking sheet, leaving about 1½ inches (4 cm) between the sausage balls (you might need to make these in batches). Bake them for 15 minutes or until golden-brown.

Place a piece of fried apple skin-side down on a platter and nestle a sausage ball in the curve of the wedge, securing it with a toothpick. Repeat with the remaining sausage balls and apple wedges and serve.

## Fried Apples

Some sweeter versions of this dish could stand in for dessert. But adding less sugar and keeping the fruit more firm allows nature's sweet-tart dance to play out.

**Makes 6 servings**

3 tablespoons butter

8 small Granny Smith apples, peel left on, cored, and sliced into ½-inch (12-mm) wedges

2 tablespoons light brown sugar

2 pinches sea salt

In a large skillet, melt the butter over medium heat. Add the apple wedges to the pan and stir to coat them with butter. Sprinkle on the brown sugar and salt. Stir again to distribute the sugar and salt and continue to stir occasionally until the apple wedges begin to soften but still hold their shape, about 15 minutes.

Use them as "boats" for cheesy sausage balls or serve them on their own.

# Kurdish Lentil Soup

- 2 tablespoons extra-virgin olive oil
- ½ large onion, chopped into ¼-inch (6-mm) dice
- 2 cloves garlic, finely chopped
- 2 carrots, chopped into ¼-inch (6-mm) dice
- 1 large stalk celery, chopped into ¼-inch (6-mm) dice
- 1 teaspoon ground turmeric
- 1 teaspoon ground cumin
- ½ teaspoon black pepper
- 2 cups (385 g) red lentils
- 5 cups (1.2 L) vegetable broth or water or a combination, plus additional water as needed
- 2 teaspoons sea salt, or to taste

  Flatbread for serving (optional)

  Cooked basmati rice for serving (optional)

The spread at the Kurdish dinner I attended in Nashville to break the Ramadan included grape leaves bulging with rice next to enchiladas and guava cake—not necessarily a melting pot but a jigsaw of proud offerings in colors and textiles that managed to fit.

The meals that break the fast each night—called Iftars—happen across town during Ramadan, the ninth month of the Islamic calendar, when Muslims worldwide fast, at home and at mosques. Nashville has the largest Kurdish population in the United States.

Most adults in the room had been without food or drink since sunrise, about sixteen hours. But then as the sun set—at 8:03 P.M.—an elder of the group presented a tray of dates sliced and stuffed with a tuft of shredded coconut. Cups of lentil soup came around, too, in fancy punch-style glasses rattling on saucers. Called *neesk*, it's a staple at Iftars but warms bodies any time of the year, served in bowls at home or Styrofoam cups at the mosque.

Eva Abdullah inspired this version of *neesk* with a visit to one of South Nashville's Kurdish markets for lentils, rice, and the lavash bread baked daily in the back of the store. To begin the soup-making process, she often puts on a pot of tea with cinnamon and cardamom before sizzling the onion and garlic.

**Makes 10 to 12 servings**

In a stockpot, heat the oil over medium. Sauté the onion, garlic, carrots, and celery until the vegetables begin to soften and the onions turn translucent, about 10 minutes. Add the turmeric, cumin, and pepper and cook, stirring, another minute. Add the lentils. Stir to coat, and then add the broth or water and the salt. Increase the heat to bring the soup to a boil, then reduce the heat to medium and simmer it for about 15 minutes, stirring occasionally. Adjust the soup for thickness if necessary by adding water. Also taste and adjust the seasoning. Serve the soup with flatbread and over rice if desired.

# Sweet Onion Bisque

Imagine the likes of Al Capone, Greta Garbo, and former presidents FDR and JFK spooning up this soup. It could have happened; all of them visited the Hermitage Hotel, where a version of sweet onion bisque has been served for more than a century. The ingredients are simple, but together they are transformed into a velvety and decadent blend.

**Makes 6 servings**

5 tablespoons (70 g) butter

4 sweet onions, chopped into ½-inch (12-mm) dice

2½ cups (600 ml) chicken broth

3 sprigs rosemary

½ cup (120 ml) heavy cream

Salt and white pepper to taste

Bacon cooked crumbled for garnish (optional)

Chopped chives for garnish (optional)

In a stockpot, heat the butter over medium and then add the onions. Reduce the heat to medium-low and allow them to cook for 1 hour, stirring occasionally, until golden. Turn the heat up to medium-high and when you start to hear the onions bubbling in the butter and juices, after about 3 minutes, add 1½ cups (360 ml) of the broth and the rosemary, and continue to simmer for 20 minutes until the liquid has reduced by about one fourth. Remove the tough rosemary stems from the pot.

Transfer the onion mixture to a blender and puree until it is smooth. Add the heavy cream and the remaining 1 cup (240 ml) of the broth and season with salt and white pepper. Heat through. Serve the bisque garnished with crumbled bacon and chives if desired.

# Atomic Yardbirds Hot Chicken Coleslaw

This adapted recipe comes from Brian Jackson, a co-chef and founding member of the Atomic Yardbirds, and a winner of the 2013 Music City Hot Chicken Festival amateur cook-off. He often serves this slaw with Nashville-style hot chicken.

Makes 8 servings

1   small head green cabbage

2   carrots

1   fennel bulb, stems and fronds removed

½   red onion

½   to ¾ cup (120 to 180 ml) mayonnaise (Brian prefers Duke's brand)

¼   cup (60 ml) cider vinegar

2   tablespoons freshly ground black pepper

Using a mandoline or food processor, chop the cabbage, carrots, fennel, and onion, then place them in a large bowl.

In a small bowl, combine the mayonnaise, vinegar, and pepper.

Add the dressing to the cabbage mixture and toss to combine. Chill the slaw for about 30 minutes before serving.

# The Coolest Coleslaw

Roger Mooking, host of the Cooking Channel's *Man Fire Food*, once told me that his favorite ingredient for cooling the palate is Greek yogurt. So in making this slaw to accompany hot chicken, I used Greek yogurt in place of sour cream and upped its proportion to match the mayonnaise.

Makes 8 servings

1   medium green cabbage, core removed

½   cup (120 ml) Greek yogurt

½   cup (120 ml) mayonnaise

2   tablespoons cider vinegar

1½   teaspoons sugar

1   teaspoon celery seeds

1   to 2 tablespoons chopped dill (optional)

Slice the cabbage into thin strips. Place it in a large bowl.

In a medium bowl, combine the yogurt, mayonnaise, vinegar, sugar, celery seeds, and dill (if you're using it).

Pour the dressing over the cabbage and toss. Refrigerate the slaw for about 30 minutes before serving.

Atomic Yardbirds Hot Chicken Coleslaw

# Hot Deviled Eggs

The spicy crumb topping dusted over these eggs serves as the white bread component of the Nashville-style hot chicken experience. The hot sauce, mustard, and cayenne blend for a layered heat, while the pickle adds snap. The inspiration for the spicy crumb topping came from a garlic toast version I read about on A Farmgirl's Dabbles blog.

**Makes 2 dozen pieces**

1   **dozen eggs**

*For the filling:*
1   **tablespoon Dijon mustard**

2½  **tablespoons mayonnaise**

3   **teaspoons cayenne hot sauce**

½   **teaspoon cayenne pepper**

2   **tablespoons minced dill pickle**

*For the garnish:*
½   **teaspoon cayenne pepper**

½   **teaspoon light brown sugar**

  **Pinch of ground cumin**

¼   **cup (30 g) bread crumbs**

1   **teaspoon vegetable oil**

  **Dill pickle rounds, cut into wedges for garnish**

  **Paprika**

Hard-cook the eggs by placing them in a saucepan, covering them with water, and bringing the water to a boil. Remove the pot from the heat and cover it. Allow the eggs to sit in the water for about 15 minutes.

*Make the filling:*
Slice the eggs lengthwise and drop the yolks into a medium bowl; arrange the egg white halves on a platter.

To the yolks, add the Dijon, mayonnaise, hot sauce, cayenne, and chopped pickle by mashing the mixture with the back of a fork. Set it aside in the refrigerator.

*Prepare the garnish:*
Combine the cayenne, brown sugar, and cumin with the bread crumbs in a small bowl. Heat the oil over medium and then toast the spiced bread crumbs for about a minute.

Fill the egg whites with the yolk mixture, top each one with a triangle of pickle and a sprinkle of paprika. Dust the eggs and platter with the spicy bread crumbs for color and crunch before serving.

# Southern-Style Picnic Potato Salad

This recipe is Southern in preparation and Julia Child in presentation. After all, we've seen our share of boring potato salad lumped into plain bowls at picnics. But taking just a bit more time to dress it up can make this mainstay salad a showpiece.

**Makes 8 servings**

|   |   |
|---|---|
| 3 | eggs, hard-cooked (see the instructions in Hot Deviled Eggs, page 54) |
| 2½ | pounds (1.2 kg) red potatoes |
| 1 | tablespoon sea salt |
| ½ | cup (120 ml) mayonnaise (I prefer Duke's) |
| 2 | tablespoons yellow mustard |
| 1 | tablespoon sugar |
| 2 | stalks celery, chopped |
| 2 | tablespoons dill pickle relish or dill pickles chopped into small dice |

Lettuce for serving

Fresh parsley sprig for garnish

Paprika for garnish

While the eggs are cooking, begin cooking the potatoes. I leave the skins on because I like the rustic-looking bits of red in the mix, but if you like a neater potato salad, then you might prefer to peel them. Place the potatoes in a stockpot and cover them with water. Add the salt and bring the water to a boil. Reduce the heat and simmer until the potatoes are tender, 15 to 20 minutes. Drain and let them cool, then cut them into ½-inch (12-mm) cubes, placing them in a bowl. Some skins will peel off during this process, and that's okay.

Chop two of the eggs and place them in a small bowl. Stir in the mayonnaise, mustard, sugar, celery, and pickles. Then add the mayonnaise mixture to the potatoes and gently toss to coat. Refrigerate the potato salad for 30 minutes to an hour.

To serve, line a wooden bowl with lettuce. Fill the bowl with potato salad and then garnish it with a sprig of parsley, slices of the remaining egg, and a few shakes of paprika.

# German Potato Salad

"Sometimes when people have lost a loved one, all you can do is take them a bowl of potato salad and tell them you're sorry." That's what writer John Egerton told my friend Drew Robinson, chef of Jim 'N Nick's Bar-B-Q. So when John passed, that's what I did. While my bowl of potato salad might not have made much difference among the trays of barbecue, beaten biscuits, and country ham brought by the many others he touched with his words, work, and advice, the gesture was specific and heartfelt. I remember John telling stories about the German immigrants in Nashville as well as the Gerst Haus, a German-style restaurant with a long history in town. So this potato salad, inspired by his stories and the restaurant, is one to remember John and for all of us who miss him.

**Makes about 6 servings**

2 ½ pounds (1.2 kg) Yukon gold potatoes, all of similar size

3 ¾ teaspoons salt

4 slices bacon

½ yellow onion, sliced

1 tablespoon all-purpose flour

½ cup (120 ml) cider vinegar

1 tablespoon sugar

½ teaspoon celery seeds

½ teaspoon Dijon mustard

2 tablespoons chopped fresh parsley

In a large stockpot, cover the potatoes with water by about 1 inch (2.5 cm) and add 3 teaspoons of the salt. Bring the water to a boil and then reduce the heat to medium and simmer for about 15 minutes or until a fork pierces them easily. Drain the potatoes. When they are cool enough to handle, slice them into thin rounds.

While the potatoes are cooking, fry the bacon, then set it aside on a paper-towel-lined plate. Sauté the onion in the bacon drippings until it is soft and brown, about 10 minutes. Add the flour to the pan and stir to combine. Then add the vinegar, sugar, celery seeds, and mustard, stirring constantly for 1 minute.

Add the potatoes and bacon, crumbled into pieces, to the pan and season them with the remaining ¾ teaspoon salt. Stir gently to coat. When the salad is heated through, transfer it to a serving bowl. Garnish it with the parsley and serve it hot or at room temperature.

# Sunshine Broccoli Salad

Inspired by the Bells Bend Farms potluck (see the story on page 180), this salad looks as much like summer as it tastes with its golden raisins, yellow bell pepper, and sunflower seeds.

**Makes about 6 servings**

- 2 small heads broccoli, cut or broken into 1-inch (2.5-cm) florets
- ½ yellow bell pepper, seeds and ribs removed, cut into strips about 1 inch (2.5 cm) long
- ½ cup (85 g) golden raisins
- 2 tablespoons roasted sunflower seeds
- ½ cup (120 ml) mayonnaise
- 2 tablespoons sugar
- 1 tablespoon cider vinegar
- ¼ teaspoon kosher salt
- ¼ teaspoon black pepper

In a medium serving bowl, combine the broccoli, bell pepper, raisins, and sunflower seeds.

In a small bowl, combine the mayonnaise, sugar, vinegar, salt, and pepper.

Add the mayonnaise dressing to the broccoli and pepper mixture and toss to coat. Cover and chill the salad for 30 minutes to an hour before serving.

# Tomato Cucumber Salad

## *with* Tahini Dressing

Many a tomato cucumber salad has been carried to the church potluck. The Nashville Food Project inspired this recipe, as it serves a similar and more modern version of the classic salad at the Trinity United Methodist community meal (more on that story on page 164).

Bowls of this dish hit the tables first, before the meal officially began, so before we had even finished plating platters of the main course, guests were already coming to the kitchen with empty bowls, asking for seconds. The many colors, variety of textures, and earthy yet bright tahini dressing make it an easy stunner.

**Makes 6 to 8 servings**

| | |
|---|---|
| 1 | pint (280 g) cherry tomatoes, halved |
| 1 | cucumber, halved and sliced, seeds removed |
| 1 | carrot, grated |
| 1½ | cups (245 g) canned chickpeas, drained and rinsed |
| ¼ | cup (60 ml) tahini |
| 2 | tablespoons lemon juice |
| ¼ | teaspoon sea salt |
| 2 | pinches sugar |
| 2 | shakes soy sauce |

In a medium bowl, combine the tomatoes, cucumber, carrot, and chickpeas.

In a small bowl, combine the tahini, lemon juice, salt, sugar, soy sauce, and 2 tablespoons water.

Add the dressing to the tomato mixture by the spoonful, tossing to coat. Serve it as you would any crisp salad—as a starter or alongside burgers, chicken, or steak.

## THE RECIPES

———

# BIRDS
# BIRDS
# BIRDS

**M**any Southerners can tell a familiar family story of not so long ago when home cooks scooped up yard birds, nicknamed for their freewheeling ways pecking behind the house, as the first unwritten step in a recipe. Even those common meals of fried chicken or chicken and dumplings were cherished for the care they took to prepare.

At bridal shower luncheons and in Nashville tearooms, cooks dressed chicken up as salad with mayonnaise and herbs. Hunters celebrated over their haul of quail, duck, and dove, and turkey keeps its role as showpiece on Thanksgiving and Christmas tables, roasted or deep fried and drizzled with gravy. Simple roasted chicken could even make for a quiet party of two over a comfortable dinner at home.

Preachers and ministers spent grateful Sundays at the homes of generous churchgoers taking first pick of the communal food, while in Nashville, the Ryman Auditorium, also known as "the mother church of country music," hosted fried chicken feeds of a different sort. Performers of the Grand Ole Opry at the Ryman say they remember the aroma of fried chicken wafting up from the pews as they played and sang. In those days, guests could pack their own supper from home.

Fried chicken also inspired Nashville-based chain restaurants for a moment, from Minnie Pearl's Chicken to Eddy Arnold's Tennessee Fried Chicken. Though few of them had the staying power of home-cooked fried chicken, a mom-and-pop place called Prince's Hot Chicken Shack added a devilish, spicy spin to fried chicken in the 1930s, and it still carries on the communal spirit and celebratory tradition of chicken after church. Hot chicken isn't just a meal, it's entertainment. It pulls us into the moment for a physical experience that's a little bit of pain mixed with a wallop of pleasure.

The recipes in this section aim to capture the spirit of coming together over poultry, no matter how small or large the gathering. The simple fried chicken recipe here can be pulled together quickly for an impromptu feast for family or friends. And Nashville's hot chicken can be turned out for a party in several forms—fried, roasted whole over potatoes, or turned into salad—proving that even leftovers of this dish are something to celebrate.

## KITCHEN PLAYLIST

These are tunes inspired by Southern birds and are ideal to play when cooking your own.

**Take an Old Cold Tater (And Wait)**
LITTLE JIMMY DICKENS

All four feet and eleven inches of Little Jimmy Dickens might have been covered in a rhinestone suit when he sang this tune, written from the perspective of a boy waiting his turn at the chicken platter as the pastor and other guests took first pick.

**There Ain't a Chicken Safe in Tennessee**
HOMER AND JETHRO

Satire songs from the "Thinking Man's Hillbillies" included this number from the heyday of the fast-food fried-chicken craze.

**Fried Chicken and a Country Tune**
BILLY EDD WHEELER

This tune links the businesses of fried chicken and country music.

**Mama Bake a Pie, Daddy Kill a Chicken**
TOM T. HALL

One of Nashville's greatest songwriters, with eleven number one hits and more than double that in the Top 10 chart, wrote this song about a soldier's welcome after returning from war.

# Nashville Hot Chicken

André Prince Jeffries carries the hot chicken torch.

In a city of stars, Nashville's hot chicken burns brightly. Fried in large black skillets and then caked in a cayenne paste, it glows orange and rusty-red, like a lump from the furnace of Hell. It arrives crispy outside and juicy inside, on a bed of white bread topped with kryptonite-green pickles. And more than just a heat thing, hot chicken stays with you. It can alter a person's state of being, drawing him back for more.

Eating hot chicken often involves ritual, too. Those who love it tend to develop a method for taking down the bird—bite of chicken, bite of pickle, bite of bread. Repeat. As the heat picks up, so does the speed, because you keep thinking you'll push through the burn until you're a sweating, stammering cartoon character, a blur of greasy fingers and arms churning in one place and desperate to escape the fire.

So, you might be thinking, why put yourself through it?

Hot chicken is more than a meal; it's an experience. It's entertainment, but also zen. It's hard to think about much else when eating hot chicken.

People go for hot chicken to celebrate birthdays and holidays. They eat it on dares and on dates. They pick it up to go, perfuming their cars on the way back to work or home with the grease-spotted brown paper sacks, and they order it blurry-eyed at two A.M. to burn off the night's alcohol.

André Prince Jeffries, the woman who has ruled the roost at Prince's Hot Chicken Shack for more than thirty years, has seen it all as customers bring all sorts of moods to the kitchen window—celebratory to feisty and tipsy.

She sees ladies of the night who want a jolt to get them in the mood, and she sees overdue pregnant women hoping the heat will induce labor (and sometimes it does). Chefs and musicians visit, as well as tourists who might arrive by cab while celebrities arrive with their agents. When Jerry Seinfeld visited, he pointed at André and said, "I've seen you on TV!"

These days you can find hot chicken on menus all across Nashville, but Prince's Hot Chicken Shack is the original. Located in a strip mall beside a nail shop with bars on the windows, it's the type of place where customers line up to order at a kitchen window between seafoam walls decorated with yellowed newspaper clippings and artwork of Michael Jackson and Jesus.

Ask André if she always had an inkling she'd go into the family business, and her answer comes without hesitation. "Heavens, no," she half shouts over the whirl of box fans and a TV in the corner that seems to perpetually play the soaps. But in 1980, her mother's dying wish was that André would take over the restaurant. So the week after her mother succumbed to breast cancer, André showed up at the chicken shack to work. She has been there nearly every day since.

As the legend goes, Prince's Hot Chicken began in the 1930s when a girlfriend of Thornton Prince (André's great-uncle) dumped extra spice on fried chicken as revenge for his cheating ways. He loved it. Thornton developed his own recipe and opened a restaurant that became a gathering place for the African-American community. In the days of segregation, the white musicians from the Opry, who also craved the spicy bird, slipped in after shows, but they had to sit in the back.

Over the years, hot chicken joints have popped up, offering their own twists in many neighborhoods. Even the country stars Lorrie Morgan and Sammy Kershaw once tried their hand at the restaurant business with a hot chicken joint. In the last decade or so, Nashville-style hot chicken has flown the coop in a big way, landing on menus from New York to Napa. Now, in addition to standbys like Bolton's Spicy Chicken and Fish and Hattie B's Hot Chicken, you'll find it on restaurant menus, from the highfalutin' version at the Catbird Seat—hot chicken skin with a tuft of white bread puree and dill pickle salt—to the Japanese-influenced hot chicken buns of Otaku South.

Hot chicken, whether dressed down or fancied up, will hardly ever be called forgettable. It will, however, make you forget all else as it places you squarely in the moment to swear, wipe a brow, fan a face, and reach for more. Hot chicken thrills as Nashville's culinary claim to fame, because both city and dish know how to put on a show.

# Fried Hot Chicken
## *on* White Bread *with* Pickle

André Prince Jeffries gave me strict orders: No sugar in the hot chicken. But I also believe part of the fun in cooking your own hot chicken comes from figuring out the spice blend you like best. And following the lead of the folks at Hattie B's, I do like a touch of brown sugar to balance out the heat.

I use red pepper flakes for texture and an added layer of spice, and I like a touch of cumin for woodsy depth. Applying the spicy paste after chicken has been fried keeps the cayenne from scorching, and it allows the cook to customize the degree of heat per piece of chicken. Go ahead and experiment to make your own blend. And apologies to Ms. Jeffries. I'll always visit Prince's to taste the original.

**Makes 4 servings**

*For the brine:*

- ½ cup (70 g) dark brown sugar
- ½ cup (120 ml) hot cayenne pepper sauce (such as Frank's RedHot)
- ¼ cup (70 g) fine kosher salt
- 1 chicken (about 3 pounds/1.4 kg), cut into 8 pieces

*For the hot coating:*

- 3 to 4 tablespoons (45 to 60 ml) vegetable oil
- 2 tablespoons cayenne pepper
- 1½ teaspoons dark brown sugar
- 1 teaspoon crushed red pepper
- ½ teaspoon garlic powder
- ½ teaspoon fine kosher salt
- ¼ teaspoon ground cumin

*For frying:*

- 2 cups (250 g) all-purpose flour
- ½ teaspoon fine kosher salt
- 1 teaspoon black pepper
- Vegetable oil for frying

*For serving:*

- 8 slices plain white sandwich bread (such as Wonder brand)
- Dill pickle rounds

*Make the brine:*
In a large stockpot, combine 5 cups (1.2 L) water, the brown sugar, hot sauce, and salt and heat the mixture over medium, stirring, just until the solids dissolve. Remove the pot from the heat and let the brine cool completely before adding the chicken to the brine. Cover and refrigerate for at least an hour, or overnight if possible.

*Make the hot coating:*
Heat the oil in a small saucepan, then add the cayenne, brown sugar, crushed red pepper, garlic powder, salt, and cumin, stirring until fragrant, about a minute, to combine the ingredients, flavor the oil, and open up the spices. Set the mixture aside.

*Fry the chicken:*
Prepare the flour for dredging by combining it with the salt and pepper in a shallow dish such as a pie plate.

Remove the chicken from the brine and pat it dry. Allow it to come up to room temperature (about 30 minutes, covered).

Pour a good amount of oil into a cast-iron skillet; it should cover the chicken about halfway once the meat is placed in the pan. Attach a thermometer to the side of the skillet and bring the temperature up to 350°F (175°C).

Quickly dredge the chicken in the flour mixture. Shake off the excess and lower the chicken, skin side down, into the oil. The temperature will drop to about 300°F (150°C) when the chicken goes into the skillet. That's okay. Don't crank the heat, but continuously adjust it up and down as you fry to keep the temperature hovering around 325°F (165°C). Be careful not to crowd the chicken—I usually fry about three pieces at a time in a 9-inch (23-cm) skillet.

Continue frying the chicken for about 10 minutes per side, turning it once using tongs. You can cover the skillet as you fry if you'd like, but leaving the lid off will make for crispier chicken, which I prefer.

Once the chicken is golden brown, transfer it to a paper-towel-lined plate to cool slightly before coating it in the spiced oil.

Arrange two pieces of white bread on each plate. Using a brush, dab hot coating mixture onto one side of the chicken. Place the pieces of chicken spiced side down on the bread slices and continue brushing the top sides with the hot coating mixture. Serve with plenty of pickles.

# Skillet-Roasted Hot Chicken

*over* Potatoes, Onion, *and* Fennel

Just about a year before you could find hot chicken variations on every corner in Nashville, I tasted the late chef Toby Willis's roasted hot chicken breast at the Nashville City Club. I adapted his version for roasting a whole chicken in an iron skillet over a bed of potatoes, red onion, and fennel that I toss with fennel fronds (and chicken drippings) just before serving.

**Makes 6 to 8 servings**

*For the marinade:*

1 quart (960 ml) buttermilk

1 cup (240 ml) hot cayenne pepper sauce (such as Frank's RedHot)

1 chicken (3 to 5 pounds/ 1.4 to 2.3 kg)

*For the spiced oil:*

½ cup (120 ml) vegetable oil

7 tablespoons (60 g) cayenne pepper

1½ teaspoons dark brown sugar

2 teaspoons dry mustard

1 teaspoon paprika

2 teaspoons kosher salt

½ teaspoon garlic powder

1 teaspoon black pepper

*For roasting:*

4 small red potatoes, quartered

1 large fennel bulb, cut into eighths (or 2 smaller ones, quartered), fronds reserved

1 medium red onion, quartered

Vegetable oil

Kosher salt

1 head garlic

Preheat the oven to 400°F (205°C).

*Make the marinade:*
In a large bowl, combine the buttermilk and hot sauce. Submerge the chicken in the mixture and refrigerate it for at least 2 hours or overnight.

*Prepare the spiced oil:*
In a small saucepan, heat the oil over medium until it shimmers. Add the cayenne, brown sugar, mustard, paprika, salt, garlic powder, and pepper and cook, stirring, until fragrant, about a minute. Divide the spiced oil between two bowls; set one bowl aside for serving.

*Roast the chicken and vegetables:*
Place the potatoes, fennel, and onion in an iron skillet. Drizzle them lightly with vegetable oil, sprinkle them with salt, and toss to coat. You want enough oil to keep the vegetables from drying out in the oven, but remember they'll also receive a lot of juice from the chicken as it cooks.

Remove the chicken from the marinade and rinse it off. Pat the chicken dry, rub it with just a bit of oil, and sprinkle it liberally with salt. Place the bird on top of the vegetables, tucking the wings under. Place the whole garlic inside the cavity. Tie the legs together with kitchen string.

Roast the chicken for about 40 minutes, until it begins to turn golden, then baste it with the spiced oil mixture using a brush. Continue roasting the chicken for another 40 to 50 minutes, basting it halfway through that time and once again at the end.

When an instant-read thermometer inserted into the inner thigh (but not touching bone) reads 165°F (74°C), the bird is done. Be aware that the juices might not run completely clear when you pierce the skin, as they're compromised by the color of the paste, so rely on the thermometer reading.

Transfer the chicken to a cutting board and allow it to cool slightly before carving.

Transfer the vegetables to a serving dish and then toss them with a tablespoon or two of chopped fennel fronds (add roasted garlic from the cavity of bird if desired).

Serve the chicken with vegetables on the side and the reserved bowl of spiced oil for drizzling.

# Leftover Hot Chicken Green Salad

## *with* Spicy White Bread Croutons

As a hot chicken fan, Emily Walters created a Facebook group called the Fraternal Order of the Hot Chicken (FOHC) for discussion and news about favorite versions around town.

Also an excellent home cook, Emily develops many of her own creations, including this salad with leftover hot chicken. The romaine and cucumber add a cool, fresh crunch while she brilliantly transforms the spicy, grease-soaked bread into croutons. She serves it with a creamy dressing, which balances out some of the heat.

For this version, I made a green goddess dressing, omitting the anchovies and some of the herbs to allow the chopped pickle to give the dressing a trademark color.

**Makes 2 to 4 servings**

1 head romaine lettuce, chopped into bite-size pieces

½ medium red onion, thinly sliced

½ medium cucumber, quartered and finely diced

2 handfuls grape tomatoes

2 cups (286 g) leftover hot chicken, removed from the bone and cut into chunks

*For the croutons:*

2 slices leftover hot chicken white bread, cut into squares

Vegetable oil, if needed

*For the dressing:*

½ cup (120 ml) sour cream

½ cup (120 ml) mayonnaise

¼ cup (81 g) dill pickles, finely chopped

1½ to 2 tablespoons lemon juice

¼ cup (10 g) fresh parsley leaves, finely chopped

¼ teaspoon black pepper

Salt, if needed

Combine the lettuce, onion, cucumber, tomatoes, and chicken in a large bowl.

*Make the croutons:*
On a baking pan covered with foil, arrange the squares of bread so that none touch. If some of them seem a little dry, you might want to toss them with vegetable oil.

Broil the croutons on low for about 10 minutes, turning them with a spatula about halfway through the cooking time to ensure that they crisp up on each side. Set them aside to cool.

*Prepare the dressing:*
In a medium bowl, combine the sour cream, mayonnaise, and pickles. Add 1½ tablespoons lemon juice, parsley, and pepper, and stir to combine. Taste and adjust the seasoning by adding salt if you'd like (but I find I don't need it with the pickle and saltiness of the chicken) or more lemon juice, if you'd like the dressing a little thinner and more tart.

Add the croutons to the salad mixture and drizzle with dressing before serving.

RATIO MIX

RAW DASHI

SZG
PEPPERCORN

GROUND
SZG PEPPERCORN

BOURBON SMOKED
PAPRIKA

Hot C

SZE MARLIAU

Green SECHUAN PEPPER

TOGARASHI MIX

Spice 6/4

Togarashi 3/25

# Otaku South's Hot Chicken Buns

"I am a spice lover," said Sarah Gavigan, who serves a version of these Nashville-style hot chicken buns at her Japanese-influenced Otaku South restaurant. "It didn't seem like a far walk from where I was with the version of fried chicken (*kara-age*) and the Chinese *bao* bun to make a hot chicken bun."

**Makes 9 hot chicken buns**

- 3 boneless, skinless chicken breasts
- 2 cups (480 ml) buttermilk
- 3 cups (720 ml) white vinegar
- Kosher salt and black pepper
- 1½ tablespoons sugar
- 1 small bunch fresh dill
- 2 teaspoons whole coriander
- ½ teaspoon ground turmeric
- 1 medium cucumber
- 2½ tablespoons dark brown sugar
- 2 tablespoons sweet paprika
- 1½ tablespoons ground guajillo chile
- 1½ tablespoons ground habañero chile
- 1½ tablespoons cayenne pepper
- 1 cup (125 g) all-purpose flour
- 1 cup (190 g) potato starch
- *Bao* buns (see Note)
- 6 cups (1.4 L) canola oil
- 2½ cups (250 g) shredded cabbage
- ¼ cup (60 ml) Kewpie mayonnaise (see Note)

*One day ahead:*
Cut the chicken breasts into nine equal pieces that are as close to rectangular as possible. Place them in a nonreactive bowl with the buttermilk to marinate overnight.

In a saucepan, bring the vinegar, 1½ tablespoons salt, 2 tablespoons pepper, the sugar, dill, coriander, and turmeric to a boil. Meanwhile, clean and slice the cucumber into ¼-inch (6-mm) slices and place them in a casserole dish. Pour the vinegar mixture over the cucumbers. Allow it to cool, then weight down the cucumbers with a plate. Refrigerate overnight.

*The next day:*
Make the hot chicken spice by combining the brown sugar, paprika, guajillo, habañero, and cayenne in a medium bowl.

Prepare the mixture for dredging the chicken by combining the flour and potato starch in a wide shallow bowl. Add salt and pepper to taste.

If you're using a bamboo steamer, add water to your wok and make sure the steam is rolling when you add the *bao* buns. They take about 7 minutes to steam from frozen, but they will hold in the steamer for up to 15 minutes.

In a skillet, heat the oil to 350°F (175°C). Pull the chicken from the buttermilk and allow it to drain. Then dredge the pieces in the flour mixture and fry until they are brown and floating in the oil, 3 to 4 minutes or until golden brown. Transfer them to a paper-towel-lined plate to drain. Then add a touch of the frying oil to the hot chicken spice and toss the fried chicken pieces in the spice.

Just before serving, prepare the slaw by combining the cabbage and mayonnaise with a touch of salt and pepper.

Assemble the buns by layering the chicken first, then add the pickles and top with the slaw. Close the buns and serve.

*Note:* Most Asian markets carry Kewpie mayonnaise, *bao* buns, and bamboo steamers.

# Hot Chicken Salad Sandwiches

Hot chicken aficionado and Nashville fine-wines manager Brent Hilton taught me this recipe while cleaning up after a party. Brent had several pieces of hot chicken left over, and when I asked what he planned to do with them, he didn't hesitate to give me instructions for the recipe below. And, given his profession, he makes great wine recommendations for pairing with hot chicken. Try a Patrick Bottex Vin du Bugey-Cerdon, Mönchhof Estate Riesling, or Tintero Moscato d'Asti. "Really any wine with residual sugar and higher acids works well with all spicy food," he says.

While you can pile this "salad" on any size roll, I recommend a choice that's somewhat smaller. The chicken and dressing make for a rich bite.

**Makes about 8 sandwiches**

2 cups (285 g) leftover hot chicken, pulled from the bone and chopped into chunks

2 tablespoons chopped dill pickle

¼ cup (60 ml) sour cream

¼ cup (60 ml) mayonnaise, plus additional for spreading

8 small to medium-size rolls

Yellow mustard

Leafy green lettuce

In a medium bowl, combine the chicken with the pickle, sour cream, and mayonnaise until coated.

Lightly toast the rolls, and then spread one side with mustard and the other side with a thin layer of mayonnaise to moisten. Pile the chicken onto the bottom half of each roll, add a piece of lettuce, and then set the top half of the roll in place before serving.

# Traditional Fried Chicken

After interviewing Thomas Keller at Prince's Hot Chicken Shack for the *Tennessean*, I decided to cook a batch of fried chicken following his recipe. Armed with its seventeen ingredients and his advice, I enlisted the help of my best friend, and we put together a party. It took two days to make the chicken. And it was perfect. A recipe I'll cook again. But I also wanted a simpler version for this book.

I believe traditional dishes like fried chicken need to be both preserved and demystified. If you've never fried chicken before, I don't want you to be afraid of doing so. This version requires few special tools or ingredients. And while you can certainly marinate it in buttermilk overnight, it's not a requirement, just as an egg wash or a brine isn't either. But it's also by no means a dumbing down in process or flavor. This is everyday fried chicken as my grandmother would have made it.

Choose a smaller bird for better frying. As for flour, you can use self-rising, but the leavening will cause it to puff up more than all-purpose. I prefer a thinner, crispier crust.

**Makes 4 to 6 servings**

1 chicken (about 3 pounds/1.4 kg)

Sea salt and black pepper

2 cups (250 g) all-purpose flour

Vegetable oil

Cut the chicken into pieces (or purchase it already cut up). Pat them dry. Season the chicken liberally with salt and pepper. Cover and allow it to come up to room temperature, 15 to 30 minutes.

Meanwhile, in a wide, shallow bowl for dredging, combine the flour with 1 teaspoon each salt and pepper.

Pour a good amount of vegetable oil into a cast-iron skillet; it should cover the chicken about halfway once the meat is placed in the pan. Attach a thermometer to the side of skillet and bring the temperature up to 350°F (175°C).

Quickly dredge a piece of chicken in the flour mixture. Shake off the excess and lower it, skin side down, into the oil. The temperature will drop to about 300°F (150°C) when the chicken goes into skillet.

That's okay. Don't crank the heat up. Just adjust it moderately up and down as you fry to keep the temperature hovering around 325°F (165°C). Be careful not to crowd the chicken. I usually fry about three pieces at a time in a 9-inch (23-cm) skillet.

Continue frying the chicken for 10 to 15 minutes per side, depending on the size of the piece and the temperature of the oil. Turn the chicken once, using tongs. You can cover the skillet as you fry if you'd like, but leaving the lid off will make for crispier chicken, which I prefer.

Transfer the chicken to a paper-towel-lined plate to cool before serving.

# Chicken and Dumplings

I trust my friend Jaime Miller's version of any dish, particularly this hearty, one-pot stew with pillows of dumplings nestled among hunks of moist chicken pulled from the bone.

**Makes 8 to 10 servings**

*For the dumplings:*

- 2 cups (250 g) all-purpose flour
- 1 tablespoon baking powder
- 1 teaspoon kosher salt
- 2 eggs
- ¾ to 1 cup (180 to 240 ml) buttermilk

*For the gravy:*

- 4 tablespoons (55 g) butter
- 2 carrots, sliced on the diagonal into ¼-inch (6-mm) pieces
- 3 medium stalks celery, sliced on the diagonal into ¼-inch (6-mm) pieces
- 2 leeks, washed and thinly sliced
- 2 cloves garlic, minced
- 2 bay leaves
- 3 tablespoons all-purpose flour
- 6 cups (1.4 L) chicken stock
- ¼ cup (60 ml) heavy cream
- 1 roasted chicken (3 to 5 pounds/1.4 to 2.3 kg), meat removed from the bone and shredded (I like breast meat for this)

  Cracked black pepper

  Chopped Italian parsley for garnish

*Prepare the dumplings:*
In a medium bowl, whisk together the flour, baking powder, and salt. In a separate small bowl, whisk together the eggs and ¾ cup (180 ml) buttermilk. Add the wet ingredients to the dry and stir just until a shaggy dough forms. Add more buttermilk if needed.

*Prepare the gravy:*
In a Dutch oven or large stockpot, melt the butter over medium heat. Add the carrots, celery, leeks, garlic, and bay leaves. Sauté until the vegetables are soft, about 5 minutes. Stir in the flour to make a roux. Continue to stir and cook for 2 to 3 minutes. Slowly pour in the chicken stock, 1 cup (240 ml) at a time, stirring well after each addition.

Let the sauce simmer until it is thick enough to coat the back of a spoon, about 15 minutes. Stir in the cream.

Fold the shredded chicken into the gravy and bring the mixture to a simmer. Using 2 spoons, carefully drop heaping tablespoons of the dumpling batter onto the hot mixture.

The dumplings should cover the top of the sauce but should not be crowded. Cook for 10 to 12 minutes uncovered until they are puffed and firm to the touch. Season with freshly cracked black pepper and garnish with parsley before serving.

# Tearoom-Style Chicken Salad Stuffed Tomatoes

I once read a rumor that a cola heiress in Atlanta was booted from a women's club for not using all white meat in her chicken salad for an event. Surely it can't be true.

Either way, chicken salad has been a staple of ladies-who-lunch tearooms and bridesmaid luncheons across the South for decades. Spooning it into a tomato adds another level of thoughtful presentation while also providing an edible vessel for the creamy concoction.

This version begins with roasting a chicken for a flavor that's deep and layered, but when pressed for time, a rotisserie chicken from the grocery deli works, too.

**Makes about 6 stuffed tomatoes**

- 1  chicken (about 3 pounds/1.4 kg)
- Olive oil
- Sea salt and black pepper
- 1  bunch thyme
- 1  lemon, cut in half
- 1  tablespoon butter
- ½  cup (50 g) pecan halves
- ⅔  (165 ml) cup mayonnaise
- ⅓  cup (80 ml) sour cream
- 1  tablespoon chopped chives
- 1  tablespoon chopped basil
- 1  tablespoon chopped tarragon
- 2  stalks celery, finely chopped
- 1  teaspoon Dijon mustard
- 6  medium, ripe tomatoes

Preheat the oven to 425°F (220°C). Dry the chicken well and then rub it with olive oil and sprinkle it liberally with salt and pepper. Place the chicken in a cast-iron skillet. Stuff the cavity with the thyme and lemon halves. Tie the legs together with kitchen string and tuck the wings under. Roast the chicken for 1 hour and 30 minutes or until an instant-read thermometer inserted in the thickest part of the breast (but not touching bone) reads 165°F (74°C) and the juices run clear. Allow the chicken to cool.

While the chicken cooks, prepare the dressing. Heat the butter in a small skillet and then add the pecans, stirring until they are fragrant and toasted, a minute or two. Let them cool. Reserve about six pecan halves for garnish and break the others into small pieces.

In a medium bowl, combine the mayonnaise, sour cream, chives, basil, tarragon, celery, mustard, and pecan pieces.

Once the chicken has cooled, pull the meat from the bone and shred it. Combine it with the desired amount of dressing and refrigerate it for at least 30 minutes to allow the flavors to come together.

Cut an opening about 1½ inches (4 cm) wide in the top of each tomato. Scoop out the membranes and seeds, saving the tomato pulp for another application. Turn the hollowed-out tomatoes upside down onto paper towels and allow them to drain for about 10 minutes. Just before filling the tomatoes, sprinkle the insides of each tomato with salt and then fill it with salad. Top with a reserved pecan half.

# Turkey Hash

Dinner at Andrew Jackson's home, the Hermitage (just outside Nashville), often included roast turkey (or chicken or pheasant) with cornbread dressing, country ham and biscuits, turnip greens, corn, and fruit pies. And for breakfast, cooks would turn the leftover meat into a rich morning meal of cream sauce holding together hunks of roast turkey pulled from the bone.

A version of turkey hash also has been served for the past hundred years to Nashvillians at the Downtown Presbyterian Church's annual Waffle Shop during the holidays. Every year, a diverse group of downtown workers, church members, and shoppers lines up to share a meal. The turkey hash makes a rich and savory accompaniment to the waffles with syrup, grits, and spiced tea or coffee.

**Makes about 6 servings**

2  tablespoons butter

½  medium onion, finely chopped

1  clove garlic, finely chopped

2  tablespoons all-purpose flour

1½  cups (360 ml) whole milk

½  teaspoon salt

¼  teaspoon black pepper

1  tablespoon chopped fresh thyme

2  cups (568 g) chopped roasted turkey

In a large skillet, heat the butter over medium. Add the onion and cook until the pieces begin to soften. Add the garlic and cook another minute. Add the flour and stir to coat for about 2 minutes. Gradually whisk in the milk, stirring continuously until the sauce reaches the consistency of gravy. Add the salt, pepper, and thyme and stir to combine. Add the turkey and heat through, stirring constantly, before serving.

# Fried Turkey

Every year on the Tuesday before Thanksgiving, country recording artist Tracy Lawrence orchestrates an event that has 6,500 turkeys bobbing in gurgling peanut oil, filling one corner of downtown Nashville with the smell of home on a holiday.

The turkey fry started in 2005 with just Tracy, his road manager, merch guy, and bus driver manning a few fryers. A decade later, more than fifty fryers get heated up at 6 A.M. in the parking lot of the Nashville Rescue Mission to cook thousands of meals for the homeless and working poor.

Tracy's fried turkey method helps lock in moisture without the aid of a brine or basting or a finicky roasting method. It also frees up the oven for cooking Thanksgiving side dishes. While he uses an injectable marinade such as Tony Chachere's, you can just use salt and pepper, as in this recipe, if you prefer.

To fry a turkey, you'll need to find a place outdoors that is uncovered and on concrete or asphalt. Make absolutely sure the turkey is completely thawed before lowering it into hot oil.

**Makes 10 to 12 servings**

1 turkey (10 to 12 pounds/4.5 to 5.4 kg), completely thawed, neck and giblets removed

About 3 gallons (11 L) peanut oil for frying

1 tablespoon kosher salt

1 tablespoon black pepper

Put the turkey in a frying basket or insert a sturdy hook with a long handle into its cavity. Place the turkey in a 30-quart stockpot and add enough oil to barely cover the bird. Remove the turkey (in the frying basket, if you're using one) from the stockpot and bring the oil to 350°F (175°C). This may take up to 1 hour.

While the oil is heating, take the turkey back out of the basket. Pat it dry and trim away any extra fat. Season it with the salt and pepper.

When the oil is hot, lower the turkey back into the pot and fry it for 30 to 45 minutes (3½ minutes per pound is a good rule of thumb). Tracy recommends testing the temperature at the bird's meatiest sections until it registers 180°F (80°C) on an instant-read thermometer. When the turkey is done, remove it from the oil and allow it to drain and rest for about 30 minutes. Carve and serve.

# THE RECIPES

---

# Bob Woods will tell you that country ham is the pinnacle of culinary excellence in this region of the upper South. And, yes, as a man who cures ham, he might be biased.

But whether for celebrations or quiet dinners at home, meats regularly anchor the meal, and in this region, that often means pork or beef.

Indeed, looking at the geographic region of Tennessee, Kentucky, Virginia, and northern Alabama and Georgia, it makes sense that the pioneers learned to preserve ham as they did in the similar climates of Italy and Spain where prosciutto and *jamón serrano* are made.

After salting pork in the cool months of November and December and then hanging it in the smokehouse as heavy-coat weather warms to light-jacket weather in the spring, the salt equalizes throughout the ham to prevent it from spoiling. "The temperature can fluctuate, as it does a lot in this region," Bob says from his Hamery shop in Murfreesboro. "But once that ham is cured, it can last two or three years. That's one reason they liked hog. Because the meat could be preserved for a long time."

Bob's ancestors traveled over the Appalachian Mountains from North Carolina to Middle Tennessee in the early 1800s. More than likely, he says, they had hogs walking alongside them.

Over the years, he has listened to customers talk about their ancestors' dependence on pork and lard for sustenance in cornbread, biscuits, and for cooking vegetables.

But growing up in Nashville, Bob also took every chance he could get to visit his grandparents' four-hundred-acre farm with about a hundred head of cattle just south of the city in Rutherford County.

Beef, though traditionally enjoyed by the more affluent, is of course more prevalent today as well. Chef Tyler Brown of the Hermitage Hotel has not only been cooking it, he's raising cattle on a farm just west of the hotel's property. His story is included here as well as dishes with German roots that can be traced back to the immigrants who settled north of downtown, giving the Germantown neighborhood its name. Many of these German families opened butcher shops near where the Nashville Union Stock-Yards operated from 1924 to 1974. Livestock corrals just blocks from downtown held cattle and hogs awaiting their exchange.

These days Tyler and his staff prepare the beef he raises, and the chef peddles it to other restaurants and meat-and-threes like Arnold's Country Kitchen—for meat loaf smothered in tomato sauce and tucked into casseroles and carved as tender roasts on holidays.

## KITCHEN PLAYLIST

This playlist celebrates favorite meat-centric main dishes.

**Burgers and Fries**
CHARLEY PRIDE

RCA released Charley Pride's first single in 1966. He's still only one of three African Americans inducted as a member to the Grand Ole Opry.

**You Can't Hurt Ham**
RICKY SKAGGS

This humorous ode to country ham celebrates its resilience despite lack of refrigeration.

**Gone Tomorrow**
LAMBCHOP

The Nashville-based band had its biggest moments in the nineties and has been associated with the alt-country movement.

**When I Dream**
COWBOY JACK CLEMENT

Clement wrote songs for people like Johnny Cash, and he produced many other artists, including Waylon Jennings, but he also performed a beautiful rendition of this song at a tribute show just a few months before his death.

# *Chef and Farmer Tyler Brown*

Tyler Brown provides food for Red Poll cattle, just as he does for the diners who visit his restaurant.

The farmhands call him "Cookie." And the name suits him, with his twirled-up handlebar mustache and white double-breasted chef's coat pulled over a happy belly. But in more recent years, as the farm workers have witnessed, the restaurant attire has often given way to Levi's and plaid button-downs, the knives to shovels and hay bales.

It started when Tyler Brown, the executive chef of the hundred-plus-year-old Hermitage Hotel downtown, had the idea to create a sustainable, period vegetable garden for the restaurant. He wanted to raise heirloom tomatoes, beans, okra, and turnips so that guests could sit at the linen-draped tables of the sepia-toned dining room and, with one bite of roasted carrot, taste the energy of the earth. More specifically, the energy of our patch of earth here in Nashville.

So the hotel made a deal with the Land Trust for Tennessee, the group that protects the historic sixty-five-acre Glen Leven Farm just four miles from downtown Nashville. About three years and many bushels of vegetables later,

the hotel discovered Double H Farms, another 250 acres just outside Nashville in Dickson County, and began raising cattle. "I can't believe I'm allowed to do this," Tyler says, watching a group of Red Poll cattle cool their hooves in a creek, a swath of green hill as backdrop.

This sort of livestock observation has become an important part of his job. The way the cattle flick their ears or drift from the pack can give clues about their health. He also knows more about this land, from the soft-shell turtles that swim in the creek to the chanterelles growing the woods.

But of course working these farms involves more than watching. He builds fences, bales hay, rotates cattle feeding areas (they're grass fed until the last few months on grain), and participates in their circle of life, from the birthing of new calves to processing a few head of cattle every twenty days or so in Paris, Tennessee.

To say that he's come a long way in a short time from finding his first cattle on Facebook would be an understatement. But Tyler explains the learning curve as simply making a "deliberate choice to be interested in it."

He harvests vegetables at Glen Leven Farm on Tuesdays and then heads out that afternoon to sell his beef at local restaurants.

"I never anticipated all this would pull me this far away from the kitchen. The journey continues to present itself, and I have to believe it's worthy. I believe it will come back around."

It already seems to be coming around in the positive feedback he hears about his beef. It's on the menu at the Hermitage Hotel's Capitol Grille, of course, as pastrami and simply as steak. But it's also formed into meat loaf at Arnold's Country Kitchen, chipped with cream on toast at Husk and fried into meatballs at City House.

Tyler will need to grow his operation some to continue ramping up his service. "But I'm more interested in what it entails to get there," he says. "That means we're involving the community."

And that's yet another goal of Tyler's—to involve more Middle Tennesseans by building a barn and event space on Double H Farms.

"We can expand our learning," he says, "when we share."

# meats

# Double H Roast Beef

Chef Tyler Brown shared the recipe for this roast, which makes use of both his farm projects, including Double H Farms beef and handfuls of fresh herbs from Glen Leven Farm for a fragrant marinade.

**Makes about 10 servings**

- 1 beef sirloin roast (4 to 5 pounds/1.8 to 2.2 kg)
- 1 tablespoon kosher salt
- Leaves from 1 bunch thyme
- Leaves from 1 bunch rosemary
- Leaves from 1 bunch chervil
- Leaves from 1 bunch parsley
- Leaves from 1 bunch tarragon
- 1 bunch chives, snipped
- 1 small head garlic, coarsely chopped
- 1 medium shallot, coarsely chopped
- 1 cup (240 ml) cider vinegar

Place the beef in a pan and rub it down with the salt.

In a food processor, combine all the herbs with the garlic, shallot, and cider vinegar to make a marinade. Rub the mixture onto the beef and allow it to marinate, refrigerated, overnight.

When you're ready to cook the meat, preheat the oven to 425°F (220°C). Remove the beef from the marinade and place it in a roasting pan. Allow the meat to come up to room temperature. Roast the meat for 50 minutes or until an instant-read thermometer inserted into the center of the roast reads 135°F (55°C).

Tent the roast with foil and let it rest for about 15 minutes. Slice it thinly to serve.

# Spiced Round

Brined beef threaded with pork fat and spiced like Christmas has long had a place on the traditional Nashville table.

President Andrew Jackson served spiced round at the Hermitage alongside roasted turkey, plum pudding, and cider. And it's listed on the lavish 1879 holiday menu of the Maxwell House Hotel. Pick up any vintage Nashville cookbook for the home cook, and you'll find recipes for it there, too.

Local butchers and the company Elm Hill Meats produced it commercially for years, but by the 2000s, the tradition had nearly faded away. Then in 2012 a couple of young butchers with Nashville roots stepped up to bring spiced round back. Chris Carter of Porter Road Butcher said, "My grandmother knew all about it." And when Chris began offering spice round over the holidays, it turned out plenty of other customers remembered it too.

Traditionally, spiced round is similar to the German *Rinderbraten* (meaning "beef roast") with pork fat stuffing and allspice, red pepper, and brown sugar. Credit for the Nashville version is linked to the German butchers who immigrated to town in the 1800s and founded meatpacking operations along the trade route to the north on the Cumberland River.

Like many great culinary creations, spiced round also came into existence as a method of preservation, to avoid waste, and to make do with what was available. Butchers would experience a run on beef around September. To manage the oversupply in the days before refrigeration, the rounds were placed in brine in a root cellar. In later fall, during hog killing season, a run on pork resulted in a surplus of pork fat.

Chris and James employ technology such as sous-vide to help speed up the process of preparing it. This recipe combines methods from vintage Nashville cookbooks such as *Nashville: 200 Years of Hospitality*, by the Tennessee Federation of Women's Clubs, Inc., as well as advice for a quicker home-cooking method from Chris and James.

Note: The beef for this dish marinates for four days, so plan accordingly.

**Makes 8 to 10 servings**

½ cup (240 g) kosher salt

1 cup (145 g) dark brown sugar

1 beef round roast (4 to 6 pounds/1.8 to 2.7 kg)

1 tablespoon ground ginger

1 tablespoon ground cinnamon

1 tablespoon ground allspice

1 tablespoon ground nutmeg

1 tablespoon freshly ground black pepper

1 teaspoon cayenne pepper

3 to 4 strips pork fat, about 1½ inches (4 cm) wide to cover roast

Combine the salt and brown sugar and rub the mixture on the roast. Set the roast in a shallow dish, cover it, and refrigerate it overnight.

In a small bowl, combine the ginger, cinnamon, allspice, nutmeg, black pepper, and cayenne. Set about a third of the mixture aside. Rub the larger quantity of spice mixture into the roast. Return the roast to the refrigerator for 3 more days, turning the meat daily and basting it with the liquid that accumulates in the dish.

Preheat the oven to 350°F (175°C). Place the meat on a roasting pan. Cover it with the pork fat. Rub the fat with the remaining spice mixture.

Roast the beef for 1 hour and 15 minutes or until an instant-read thermometer inserted into the center reads 140°F (60°C) for medium-rare.

Let the beef rest for about 15 minutes, then slice and serve it warm. Or to serve it in the traditional style, wrap it in foil and refrigerate it; serve it cool, sliced thinly, with small biscuits.

GUEST CHECK

Date | Table | Guests | Server
APPT · SOUP/SAL · ENTREE · VEG/POT · DESSERT · BEV
0368812

RINDER BRATEN
· SPICE ·

1.5 CUPS SALT
.25 CUPS BLACK PEPPER
.25 CUPS WHITE PEPPER
.25 CUPS BROWN SUGAR
2 TBLS GINGER
2 TBLS CINNAMON
1 TBL CLOVE
1 TBL NUTMEG
1 TBL ALLSPICE

Tax
Total
— Please Come Again

Customers brought in newspaper clippings of
advertisements to Chris Carter and told stories
about eating spiced round years before.

# Beef Brisket

*with*
## Blue Cheese Grits

This simple recipe for brisket cooks down slowly in a rich broth of balsamic vinegar and red wine before being sliced and served over a bed of blue cheese grits.

**Makes 8 to 10 servings**

*For the brisket:*

4  pounds (1.8 kg) beef brisket

1  tablespoon kosher salt

2  teaspoons black pepper

3  tablespoons extra-virgin olive oil

2  large yellow onions, roughly chopped

6  to 8 carrots, cut into chunks

6  large cloves garlic, roughly chopped

½  cup (120 ml) balsamic vinegar

3  cups (720 ml) beef stock

1  cup (240 ml) red wine

4  sprigs rosemary

2  bay leaves


*For the grits:*

1  teaspoon kosher salt

2  cups (340 g) grits

1  tablespoon butter

⅓  cup (80 ml) half-and-half

¼  cup (30 g) crumbled blue cheese

Preheat the oven to 350°F (175°C).

*Prepare the brisket:*
Season the beef with the salt and pepper.

In a large Dutch oven, heat the oil over medium-high and brown the brisket on all sides. Transfer it to a plate.

Add the onions, carrots, and garlic to the pot and cook until they are softened, about 15 minutes. Add the vinegar and scrape up any bits on the bottom of the pan, and then add the beef stock, wine, rosemary, and bay leaves. Return the beef to the pot. Cover the pot and braise the beef in the oven until tender, about 3 hours, turning it every 45 minutes.

*Prepare the grits:*
In a medium saucepan, bring 6 cups (1.4 L) water to a boil. Add the salt. Add the grits, stirring, and bring the mixture to a simmer over low. Cover and continue to simmer for 20 to 30 minutes, stirring regularly. Remove the pot from the heat, and stir in the butter, half-and-half, and blue cheese until the desired consistency is reached.

When ready to serve, remove the brisket from the pot and allow to rest before slicing into pieces against the grain. Spoon a portion of the grits onto each plate and top with slices of meat and a couple spoonfuls of the cooking liquid, carrots, and onions.

# Bacon-Wrapped Meat Loaf

This meat loaf is chock-full of vegetables, adding texture and color. The bacon slices draped on top help lock in moisture as the meat cooks, and the ketchup glaze gives it that sweet familiar taste.

**Makes 1 loaf, 4 to 6 servings**

*For the loaf:*

| | |
|---|---|
| 1 | tablespoon extra-virgin olive oil |
| 1 | carrot, diced |
| ½ | onion, chopped |
| ¼ | cup (35 g) chopped green bell pepper |
| ½ | cup (65 g) chopped red bell pepper |
| 2 | cloves garlic, finely chopped |
| 1 | pound (455 g) ground beef |
| 1 | large egg |
| 1 | tablespoon chopped fresh thyme |
| 3 | tablespoons chopped fresh parsley |
| 2½ | slices white bread, torn |
| 1 | tablespoon Worcestershire sauce |
| ½ | teaspoon sea salt |
| ½ | teaspoon black pepper |
| 2 | slices bacon |

*For the sauce:*

| | |
|---|---|
| ⅓ | cup (80 ml) ketchup |
| 1½ | tablespoons brown sugar |
| 1 | teaspoon yellow mustard |

*Prepare the loaf:*
Preheat the oven to 375°F (190°C).

In a medium skillet, heat the oil over medium-high and then sauté the carrot, onion, bell peppers, and garlic until they are beginning to soften, about 10 minutes.

In a medium bowl, combine the vegetable mixture with the ground beef, egg, thyme, parsley, bread, Worcestershire, salt, and pepper. Mix the ingredients by hand just until they come together, being careful not to overwork them.

In a shallow dish, form the meat mixture into a loaf and top with the strips of bacon. Bake it for 30 minutes.

*Meanwhile, make the sauce:*
In a small bowl, combine the ketchup, brown sugar, and yellow mustard. After the meat loaf has baked for 30 minutes, brush it with the ketchup mixture. Bake it for an additional 30 minutes or until the temperature of the meat loaf reaches 160°F (70°C). Slice it into 1-inch (2.5-cm) portions to serve.

# The Nashville Burger

At Brown's Diner, one of Nashville's most beloved burger joints, bar customers must climb onto worn and wobbly stools mounted onto a low step. It's sort of a commitment. But one that's worth it for the conversations and burgers alone—grilled patty on plain bun, American cheese oozing from its edges, and pickles secured with a toothpick on top.

Then, on the other side of the Vanderbilt campus, sits another favorite burger haunt called Rotier's.

Ask Margaret Rotier what makes the famed burgers on French bun so irresistible, and she might say the freshly ground meat or the sixty-plus-year-old griddle. And she's not taking any chances on either. "We're scared to get a new one," she says of the old flat top. "It's not beautiful, but it works."

Jimmy Buffett holed up in these booths to write songs when he lived in Nashville, and while he hasn't admitted that there's one particular burger that inspired his "Cheeseburger in Paradise," the liner notes to his box set, *Boats, Beaches, Bars and Ballads,* certainly includes Rotier's as one of his ten favorite joints.

Inspired by the burgers at Rotier's and Brown's, the classic burger below, has tried-and-true toppings and French bread bun made famous by Rotier's.

**Makes 4 burgers**

1 French baguette, cut into 4 portions

2 tablespoons butter, melted

1 pound (455 g) 80% lean ground beef

Salt and black pepper

4 slices American cheese

Lettuce

Dill pickle rounds

Mayonnaise

White onion, thinly sliced

Tomato, thinly sliced

Yellow mustard

Heat a grill to medium-high. Split each piece of bread and brush the insides with melted butter.

Divide the meat into four equal portions and shape each one into an oblong patty slightly larger than your bun size using a few swift motions. Do not overwork the meat and avoid UFOs, as Porter Road Butcher's Chris Carter calls them: that is, the shape that makes patties thicker in middle than on the ends. To help avoid this, make an indentation in the middle of each burger. That way, as the burger expands during grilling, it will puff up into a flat shape. If the meat has been refrigerated, allow the patties to sit, covered, to come up to room temperature.

Just before placing patties on the grill, sprinkle them with salt and pepper—you'll need nothing more. Grill the burgers for 5 minutes with the lid up. This will give you a nice crispy outer layer. Don't press on the patties with a spatula; that will just release juices into the flames that you want to keep inside the meat. Then, turn down the heat to medium and flip the burgers. Close the grill lid and cook them for 5 minutes longer.

During the last couple of minutes of cooking, place the bread, buttered sides down, onto a cooler part of grill to toast.

Transfer the grilled patties and bread to a platter. Immediately top each patty with a slice of cheese to melt. The meat should be charred on the outside, moist and juicy inside, and a little pink—but not too much—in the center.

Stack burgers with desired condiments on the bread and serve.

# Tandy's Pork Sausage

Chef Tandy Wilson spent some time in Napa at Tra Vigne and traveled through Italy before coming home to open his rustic Italian restaurant, City House, and the food reflects his native Nashville roots with his time in Italy in dishes such as this easy sausage sauté.

**Makes 6 servings**

Peanut oil for sautéing

6 pork sausage links (about 3 ounces/ 78 g per link)

1 lemon, thinly sliced

½ red onion, thinly sliced

¼ cup (25 g) chopped Italian parsley leaves

1 apple, cored and sliced

Preheat the oven to 425°F (220°C).

Heat a large oven-proof skillet over medium. Add enough oil to film the bottom of the pan and follow it with the sausages. Cook them until they are golden brown on one side, flip the sausage, and then put them in the oven for 7 to 10 minutes until browned. Set them aside.

In a sauté pan, heat 1 tablespoon oil over medium. Distribute the lemon slices on the bottom of the pan and then layer on the onion. Cook for 3 minutes. Add the parsley and apple, remove the pan from the heat, and fold the ingredients together.

To serve, place the sausages atop the lemon-apple mixture.

# Pat's Pork Chops

*with*
## Peach Chutney

Pitmaster Pat Martin of Martin's Bar-B-Que Joint likes to encourage friends to chill out when cooking. Too often he sees people making it too hard. "I see so many people who want to cook, but they're just miserable. They're so stressed out about it. I think people should just have fun cooking."

This recipe harkens back to the days when he first took an interest in cooking and began hanging around the grill with family.

**Makes 2 servings**

*For the glaze:*

- 1 cup (240 ml) peach preserves
- 1 tablespoon soy sauce
- 1 teaspoon chili powder
- 1 teaspoon cayenne pepper
- 1 tablespoon light molasses

*For the rub:*

- 2 tablespoons kosher salt
- 1 tablespoon light brown sugar
- 1 tablespoon coarsely ground black pepper
- 1 teaspoon paprika

*For grilling the chops:*

- ½ lime per chop
- 1 tablespoon oil per chop
- 2 bone-in pork chops, 2 inches (5 cm) thick, preferably a heritage breed such as Berkshire or Duroc

*Prepare the glaze:*
In a saucepan, mix together the peach preserves, soy sauce, chili powder, cayenne, and molasses. Bring the mixture to a boil, reduce the heat to low, and simmer for 20 minutes, stirring occasionally. Allow the glaze to cool.

*Prepare the chops:*
In a small bowl, combine the salt, brown sugar, black pepper, and paprika. Rub the spice mixture onto the chops on both sides and allow them to come to room temperature.

Start the fire for your grill using a chimney starter. Do not use lighter fluid. Allow 30 minutes to heat up. Or, heat a gas grill to high. (Pat prefers the charcoal method, but we've included gas grill instructions as well.)

When the coals are ready, dump them in your grill. Add an additional two handfuls of raw charcoal on top and allow it to burn for 15 minutes. Then, pile coals to one side, leaving about half of the grill with no coals.

Squeeze lime on both sides of the pork chops and then oil the pork chops on each side.

When the coals are covered with gray ash and the fire is really hot, put the chops on the grill directly over the coals.

After 2 minutes, flip the chops and cook them for 2 additional minutes.

Move the pork chops to the part of the grill with no coals. If using a gas grill, turn off one of the burners or move the chops to cooler part of the grill. Brush them with some of the glaze. Close the lid and continue to cook the chops for 6 to 8 minutes longer, flipping and recoating them with glaze midway through.

Apply one more coat of glaze, then allow the pork chops to rest for 5 minutes at room temperature before serving.

Tandy Wilson (left) of City House restaurant and Pat Martin of Martin's Bar-B-Que Joint cook in different styles but demonstrate the comaraderie in Nashville.

# Shepherd's Pies

## *for* Loretta *and* Tammy

Country legends Loretta Lynn and Tammy Wynette both have cookbooks, and they both have beef casseroles—Loretta's "You Ain't Woman Enough" casserole to Tammy's "Husband Delight." While their dishes both call for sliced potatoes or noodles, I turned my beef casserole into more of a shepherd's pie with mashed potatoes piled on top.

**Makes 6 servings**

*For the potatoes:*
- 2 pounds (910 g) Yukon gold potatoes, peeled and cut into cubes

  Fine sea salt

- 4 tablespoons (55 g) butter
- ½ cup (120 ml) whole milk

*For the filling:*
- 1 tablespoon extra-virgin olive oil
- ½ large onion, chopped
- 1 large carrot, chopped
- 1 large stalk celery, sliced lengthwise and chopped
- 2 cloves garlic, chopped
- 1 pound (455 g) ground beef (or lamb or a mix of beef and lamb)
- 1 heaping teaspoon fresh thyme·
- ½ cup (120 ml) beef broth
- 1 (15-ounce/425-g) can diced tomatoes

- 2 teaspoons Worcestershire sauce
- 1 cup (135 g) frozen peas
- ½ teaspoon sea salt
- ½ teaspoon black pepper

*For the assembly:*
- 9 tablespoons (70 g) sharp cheddar cheese, shredded

Preheat the oven to 400°F (205°C).

*Make the potatoes:*
In a large stockpot, cover the potatoes with water, add 1 tablespoon salt to the water, and bring to a boil. Reduce the heat to simmer and cook until it's easy to pierce the potatoes with a fork, about 15 minutes. Drain the potatoes, return them to the pot, and mash them with the butter and milk until combined and smooth. Season with additional salt to taste.

*Make the filling:*
In a medium Dutch oven or large oven-safe skillet, heat the oil over medium-high. Add the onion, carrot, celery, garlic, and beef. Sauté until the meat is browned and the vegetables are softening, about 15 minutes.

Drain off the fat and add the thyme, broth, tomatoes, and Worcestershire. Simmer until the mixture starts to thicken, about 15 more minutes. Then add the peas, salt, and pepper and remove the pan from the heat.

Assemble the pies by spooning the filling into six 4-inch-by-2-inch (10-cm-by-5-cm) ramekins or small soufflés and top each with mashed potatoes; place the ramekins on a parchment-lined baking pan.

Top the potato with shredded cheese and bake for 20 minutes or until the cheese is melted and the pie is bubbling. Allow pies to cool for 10 minutes before serving.

# Chiles en Nogada
## (Stuffed Chiles *in* Walnut Sauce)

Karla Ruiz grew up near Mexico City and came to Nashville at age twenty-five with her young son. She brought her grandmother's recipes with her, and she took a job with Martha Stamps, a Nashville native and one of the city's most beloved chefs, at Belle Meade Plantation.

She learned which ingredients from her home cuisine grow well here, like tomatillos, poblanos, and jalapeños. She stuffed empanadas with kale and potatoes or with peaches and incorporated Southern ingredients into her Mexican dishes, adding peppers to cheese grits.

*Chiles en nogada,* considered a special dish prepared for royalty and singular occasions, also represents the colors of the Mexican flag, with its red pomegranate, green peppers, and white sauce. Karla says it is one of most distinctive dishes of her native country, along with tamales and slow-cooked pork.

**Makes 12 servings**

*For the stuffed peppers:*
- 4 tablespoons (55 g) butter
- ½ cup (120 ml) extra-virgin olive oil
- 4 cloves garlic, minced
- 1 yellow onion, chopped
- ¼ pound (115 g) ground pork
- ½ pound (225 g) ground beef
- ¼ pound (115 g) ground lamb
- ½ cup (85 g) raisins
- ½ cup (110 g) prunes, finely chopped
- ½ cup (110 g) candied citron, finely chopped
- ½ cup (65 g) dried apricots, finely chopped
- 2 pears, cored, peeled and finely chopped
- 2 peaches, peeled, pitted, and finely chopped
- 1 apple, peeled, cored, and finely chopped
- ½ plantain, finely chopped
- 1 tablespoon ground cinnamon
- ½ teaspoon ground cloves
- Pinch ground nutmeg
- ½ cup (120 ml) dry sherry
- Kosher salt
- 12 poblano peppers, roasted, seeded, and deveined

*For the sauce and finish:*
- 2 cups (200 g) shelled walnuts
- 7 ounces (200 g) cream cheese
- 3 ounces (85 g) soft goat cheese
- 1 tablespoon light brown sugar
- 1 cup (240 ml) heavy cream
- ½ cup (120 ml) whole milk
- 1 teaspoon ground cinnamon
- ¼ cup (60 ml) dry sherry
- Kosher salt (optional)
- Seeds of 1 pomegranate
- Parsley, chopped, for garnish

*Prepare the stuffed peppers:*
Heat the butter and oil in a saucepan over medium-high and then add the garlic, onion, and ground meats and sauté until the meats brown. Reduce the heat to medium and stir in the raisins, prunes, citron, apricots, pears, peaches, apple, and plantain and cook until the mixture begins to soften, about 25 minutes.

Add the cinnamon, cloves, nutmeg, and sherry, stirring constantly for about 10 minutes. Taste and add salt if desired.

Allow the stuffing to cool. Slice the peppers lengthwise and fill with a spoonful of the meat mixture. Place the chiles seam-side down on a platter to keep secure.

*Prepare the sauce:*
Place the walnuts in a saucepan and cover them with water. Bring to a boil and boil the nuts for about 5 minutes to soften. Drain the nuts and place them in a food processor with the cream cheese, goat cheese, brown sugar, cream, milk, cinnamon, and sherry. Whirl until smooth. Taste and add salt if desired.

Place the peppers on individual plates. Top each one with a stripe of the walnut sauce and garnish with pomegranate seeds and chopped parsley.

# Country Ham

In Bob Woods's shop, hams hang without refrigeration, and his office walls are bedecked with primitive-looking farm tools. But to those who have been around this type of thing, it's a natural part of farm life.

Bob took over his uncle and cousin's business in 1981, and these days he cures about 2,800 hams a year. His regular customers include the custodian at the courthouse, who comes for a ham once a year at the holidays, as well as top restaurant clients from Nashville to Chicago who might choose his Tennshootoe, aged and thinly sliced like prosciutto.

But one of his greatest achievements is teaching a younger generation about the tradition of curing country hams. Each year in January, he mentors a group of 4-H students aged ten to fifteen, having each one choose a ham to tag, salt, hang, smoke, and check on throughout the winter.

Artisans like Bob took care of the time and hard work for this recipe. Just be sure to make the most of what's left in the pan after frying this ham by making Redeye Gravy (page 23) to go with it.

**Makes 4 servings**

1 pound (455 g) country ham, sliced ¼ inch (6 mm) thick

Redeye Gravy (page 23)

Biscuits (page 26)

Rinse the ham to remove some of the surface salt and pat it dry. Trim away any rind or dark spots on the outer edge of the meat, but leave the fat. Slice the fat in a few places to help reduce the curling up that can happen during frying.

Heat a large cast-iron skillet over medium-high. Add the ham and fry it for 5 minutes on each side until it is browned in places and crisp on both sides. If the pan starts to smoke too much during cooking, reduce the heat to medium.

Transfer the ham to a plate and reserve the drippings for making redeye gravy. Serve it warm or room temperature with the gravy and biscuits.

# RC Cola Baked Ham

Chef Trey Cioccia of the Farm House grew up on a Middle Tennessee farm, and he likes making a ham similar to this one at home for holidays and tailgate parties. With a salty-sweet contrast that hits just the right notes, it's appropriate for breakfast, lunchtime sandwiches, or on its own at potlucks.

**Makes about 12 servings**

*For the brine:*

- 1 teaspoon black peppercorns
- 1 tablespoon mustard seeds
- 1 teaspoon allspice berries
- 2 bay leaves
- 2 cinnamon sticks
- 1 teaspoon whole cloves

  Peel from half an orange

- 7 ounces (200 g) kosher salt
- 4 quarts (3.8 L) boiling water
- 10 ounces (280 g) light brown sugar
- 2 cloves garlic, smashed
- 3 sprigs thyme
- 1 bone-in pork shoulder roast, picnic cut (9 pounds/4 kg)

*For the glaze:*

- 1 cup (240 ml) cane syrup (Trey prefers Steen's brand)
- 1 (12-ounce/355-ml) can RC Cola
- ¼ cup (35 g) light brown sugar
- ½ cup (50 g) chopped rosemary
- 2 tablespoon black pepper

*Prepare the brine:*
In a stockpot, combine the peppercorns, mustard seeds, allspice berries, bay leaves, cinnamon sticks, cloves, orange peel, salt, boiling water, brown sugar, and garlic. Bring the mixture to a boil, stirring to dissolve the sugar and salt. Allow the brine to cool, then add the thyme.

Place the pork in the cooled brine and refrigerate, covered, overnight.

The next day, take the pork out of the brine, place it on a roasting pan skin side up, and pat it dry. Score skin in crisscross pattern. Preheat the oven to 325°F (95°C).

*Prepare the glaze:*
In a pot, combine all the glaze ingredients and bring the mixture to a simmer while stirring until all the ingredients are well mixed. Let the liquid cook at a high simmer until the glaze has reduced by 25 percent. Pour about one-third of the glaze into a separate pot. (The larger pot will be used for glazing.) Keep both pots of glaze warm on the stovetop.

*Bake the ham:*
Brush the ham with the glaze and bake for about 4 hours or until the center reaches 140°F (60°C), glazing the ham at least every 30 minutes during the cooking time.

Once the ham is done, allow it to rest for about 10 minutes at room temperature before slicing. Serve it with the remaining hot glaze on the side.

# Venison Chili

Brian Jackson's award-winning chili pie helped him claim the East Nashville cooking contest trifecta in 2013 by winning first place in the 3 Crow Bar chili cook-off, the Tomato Art Fest Bloody Mary competition, and tying for first at the Music City Hot Chicken Festival's amateur cook-off.

I've melded his version of chili with my own favorite, including a sweet touch of brown sugar and red wine along with the heat of spicy sausage and jalapeño.

**Makes about 10 servings**

*For the chili:*
- ½ pound (225 g) hot sausage
- 1 pound (455 g) venison (I used saddle meat cut into bite-size cubes, but you can also use ground venison or beef)
- 2 cups (240 g) chopped onion
- 1 cup (134 g) chopped green bell pepper
- 4 cloves garlic, chopped
- 1½ tablespoons chili powder
- 2 tablespoons dark brown sugar
- 1½ tablespoons ground cumin
- 1 teaspoon dried oregano
- 2 bay leaves
- 1 (28-ounce/794-g) can whole tomatoes, coarsely chopped, liquid reserved
- 1 (28-ounce/794-g) can crushed tomatoes
- 1 (15-ounce/425-g) can dark red kidney beans, drained
- 1 (15-ounce/425-g) can light red kidney beans, drained
- 1½ cups (360 ml) red wine
- 1½ teaspoons sea salt

*For the cornbread topping:*
- 1½ cups (205 g) self-rising cornmeal
- 1 cup (240 ml) buttermilk
- ¼ cup (60 ml) vegetable oil
- 1 large egg
- 1 tablespoon bacon fat, melted
- 1 jalapeño pepper, seeds and ribs removed, finely chopped (optional)

*Prepare the chili:*
Heat a large Dutch oven over medium-high. Add the sausage and venison and begin to brown them. After a couple minutes, add the onion, bell pepper, and garlic and cook, stirring, until the meat is browned.

Add the chili powder, brown sugar, cumin, oregano, and bay leaves and cook, stirring, for a minute. Then add the canned tomatoes with their juices, the beans, wine, and salt. Bring the chili to a boil and then reduce the heat to simmer for about 1 hour.

*Prepare the cornbread topping:*
Preheat the oven to 400°F (205°C). Whisk together the cornmeal, buttermilk, oil, egg, bacon fat, and, if you're using it, the jalapeño. Carefully spoon the batter over the top of the chili. Bake the dish for 35 to 40 minutes or until a toothpick inserted into the middle of the cornbread comes out clean.

Serve the chili warm in bowls.

Venison Chili topped with cornbread.

*meats*

119

# Beer-Braised Pork Ribs

The meat from these pork ribs falls easily from the bone after it is cooked slowly in vinegar and beer. Serve this dish with crusty bread for sopping up the rich broth. The day after cooking, the shredded pork tastes great piled onto plain white sandwich bread with a swipe of mayo.

**Makes about 6 servings**

- 4 pounds (1.8 kg) bone-in, country-style pork ribs
- 2 teaspoons kosher salt
- 1 teaspoon black pepper
- 2 tablespoons extra-virgin olive oil
- 3 medium onions, quartered
- 2 large carrots, cut on the diagonal into bite-size chunks
- 4 cloves garlic, chopped
- 1 teaspoon finely chopped rosemary
- ⅔ cup (165 ml) cider vinegar
- 1 (12-ounce/355-ml) bottle amber beer (I use Yazoo Gerst)
- 2 bay leaves
- Crusty baguette for serving

Preheat the oven to 350°F (175°C).

Season the ribs with 1 teaspoon of the salt and the black pepper. In a Dutch oven, heat the oil over medium-high. Add the ribs and sear them for about 2 minutes per side. Transfer the meat to a plate.

Add the onions, carrots, and garlic to the pot. Reduce the heat to medium and cook for 2 minutes, stirring, then add rosemary and cook another minute, stirring. Add the vinegar and deglaze the pan, scraping up any bits that are stuck to the bottom. Then add the beer, bay leaves, and remaining 1 teaspoon salt.

Return the pork to the pot, along with any juices that have accumulated on the plate, and add enough water to barely cover the ribs. Cover the pot and place it in the oven. Braise the pork until it is tender, about 1½ hours, turning the ribs twice during the cooking process.

Serve the meat with hunks of crusty bread for soaking up the sauce.

# THE RECIPES

———

# FISH
## FISH
### FISH

# When you think of fish dishes in the South, crawfish tails dunked in butter might come to mind, or New Orleans gumbo in caramel-colored roux. But in landlocked Nashville, we look to the nearby lakes and rivers for our fishes.

Like other Southerners who grew up freshwater fishing, my father recalls standing in a stream holding on to his father's back pockets. He learned from an early age to spot the type of fly hatching on the water, to carefully catch it, and to take it home and replicate it with a rainbow of threads and feathers. After decades of experience, he can call pockets like a pool shark—except in his case, it's pools of water near rocks that he knows hold trout.

Chef Matt Bolus of the 404 Kitchen in Nashville remembers fishing expeditions to the streams, too, during his college years. He would make the trek toward the mountains with friends, stopping for bacon at Allan Benton's Smoky Mountain Country Hams afterward and at the A&W Root Beer drive-in restaurant. Matt says such experiences bring a person closer to an ingredient and also reinforce the value of freshness. "It's like growing your own tomato and eating it," he says.

For many others, it's the lakes that call, with their quiet, calm waters, and the contemplative time between reeling in catfish, crappie, or freshwater bass.

Several recipes in this section reflect those times on the water. Matt's trout is simply pan-fried and brightened with lemon. A smoked trout is tucked into a dip for spreading onto a cracker with a dab of hot sauce. Grilled trout and freshwater bass join fried catfish and crappie served with hushpuppies or wrapped in tortillas as tacos.

After the catching and cooking comes the eating, and it's often a communal affair. The stories here tell of hot fish piled with pickles and onions and striped with yellow mustard and hot sauce as well as a catfish fry in the spirit of a Red Barn Roundup—music and potluck gathering in East Nashville.

Fish fries happen at Elks lodges, church fund-raisers, and high school football games. One of the basketball coaches at Stratford High School often brings in his haul for a tailgate party before the games. For decades, the band boosters have been raising money selling their fried fish during games. It's an event to look forward to and celebrate, no matter which team wins.

## KITCHEN PLAYLIST

Country songs with fishing lyrics are easy to come by, but here are a few favorites, plus one homage to catfish from Jimi Hendrix, who spent time here in the 1960s.

**Fish and Whistle**
JOHN PRINE

Off John Prine's fifth album, *Bruised Orange*, this song talks about fishing in the afterlife.

**Catfish Blues**
JIMI HENDRIX

Jimi Hendrix honed his craft in the blues bars of Jefferson Avenue in Nashville.

**Pray for the Fish**
RANDY TRAVIS

A song about a river baptism of a particularly sinful man includes the preacher's request to his congregation to say a prayer not for the man but the fish.

**Southern Flavor**
OFF THE WAGON

Seattle native and fish lover Grant Johnson plays lap steel in this Nashville band, and they sometimes cover this Bill Monroe tune. For more on his fried catfish, see page 130.

# The Red Barn Roundup

Lucille the hound dog signals the start of music following a potluck fish fry.

The romantic notion of a musician arriving in Nashville by Greyhound bus, guitar over one shoulder and a duffel bag of dreams over the other, sounds like a made-for-TV moment.

But take a seat at the downtown bus station, and you'll likely spot a guitar in less than thirty minutes. After all, packing it up for Nashville has worked for many. In his memoir, Tom T. Hall tells how he drove over the city line with everything he owned in his car while shouting, "Are you ready for me, you big son of a bitch?" He went on to write many hit songs and earned the nickname "the Storyteller" for his writing style.

People who move here don't have to wait long to connect with others who made similar journeys, and they might find success in ways they didn't expect. The songwriters, designers, recording engineers, publicists, booking agents, managers, and businesspeople don't just shape the music scene with their sounds and talents.

They bring bits of home with them—food preferences and tastes—and they influence how food is prepared and enjoyed.

Steve Dale, for example, came here from New Mexico to play bass with Little Big Town. He honed his recipes for salsas and other New Mexican fare on the road by throwing after-show fiestas for the crew. Then in 2010, he opened a restaurant, Sopapilla's, just south of Nashville in Franklin, Tennessee. There he educates his customers about sauces made with Hatch chiles as well as sopapillas, pillows of fried dough and the restaurant's namesake, glistening with honey.

Beyond the restaurants, vans, tour buses, and backstage dressing rooms, the meals at home—and thus casual house parties with live music—influence and cultivate the food and tunes.

Kathryn Johnson and Allison Marusic, for example, started the Red Barn Roundup in East Nashville as a nod to the old country-music barn-style parties, where people gathered to hear bands outside of the smoky bars and high-priced concert halls. Having a party at Allison's house on Sunday afternoons meant musicians who stayed up until the wee hours could come, as well as nine-to-five folks, neighbors, and kids. It naturally evolved into a potluck, too.

"Allison and I never officially planned on the potluck aspect of the Red Barn Roundup," Kathryn says. "But being the nature of the South and our friends, no one wanted to come empty-handed, and we always put out a few snacks—usually some little biscuits, cookies or bars, a pie or two, and some veggies with a dip—and everyone followed suit."

Kathryn says many of her friends come from other parts of the country and bring dishes that reflect their various homes—a pot of gumbo from a New Orleans native, say, or a West Virginian's spicy meat pie. Kathryn often makes mini biscuits with apple and cheddar (page 21) as

a snack, and her friend Rebekah Turshen, pastry chef at City House restaurant, will bring plates of oatmeal cookies and an old family favorite, Hello Dolly bars (page 214), which are easy to grab on the way to watch the band's set.

And while Allison really does have a red barn-style shed beside her house, giving it the Red Barn Roundup name, Kathryn also hosts band practices with her musician-husband, Grant, at their home. On one potluck night, he dunked catfish fillets into buttermilk and fried chicken batter and dropped them sizzling into cast iron for a laid-back fish fry.

"Fish was our life growing up," he says. Living in a Scandinavian neighborhood in Seattle with a Swedish father and Norwegian mother, he would go crabbing or salmon fishing in the fall and would take his catch directly to be smoked and canned. "Moving here, I needed some sort of fish in my life."

Grant's bandmate from Indiana, Nate Shuppert, said that the music scene makes for a culinary melting pot of sorts, even if it looks less exotic at times, with its blending of Midwestern pies and California-style tacos with a love for

barbecue. "Once you move here, you come to embrace all the Southern traditions like smoking meats and no sugar in cornbread," he says.

Songwriter Jacob Jones came to Nashville after a stint in New York City. He arrived with little money and lots of tattoos, and he tended bar in addition to playing shows. But he ended up creating a Monday night soul dance party that *GQ* magazine dubbed the "most stylish" dance party in the country, leading to a marketing and branding business he runs called Mountain. Nowadays, he's more apt to wear a suit on occasion.

"My mom especially liked to make this pie in the summer," Jacob says of his blueberry pie, a potluck offering with Midwestern roots. "She had a garden and small farm growing up, with fruit trees and rhubarb."

And so as slices were handed out, blueberries staining the fluffy whipped cream, the bluegrass began to drift up from the patio, and Lucille the hound dog howled as if inviting the group down to check it out. The music, after all, is still what got this crowd together in the first place.

Grant Johnson dunks catfish fillets into buttermilk and fried chicken batter and then drops them into a sizzling cast-iron pan.

# Grant's Nashville Pan-Fried Catfish

Grant Johnson, a guitarist who moved to Nashville for the music, craves the fish he grew up eating in Seattle. He makes this catfish recipe using a recipe for breading that he learned for fried chicken.

**Makes 2 to 4 servings**

- 1 cup (125 g) all-purpose flour (Grant prefers White Lily brand)
- 1 cup (120 g) medium-grind cornmeal (Grant prefers Falls Mill brand)
- 1 tablespoon sea salt
- 1 teaspoon black pepper
- 1 heaping teaspoon garlic powder
- 1 heaping teaspoon chili powder
- ½ teaspoon cayenne pepper (or more if you want it hot)
- 1 large egg
- 1 cup (240 ml) buttermilk
- Grapeseed oil for frying
- 2 to 4 pieces catfish

In a medium shallow bowl, mix the flour, cornmeal, salt, pepper, garlic powder, chili powder, and cayenne.

In a second medium shallow bowl, whisk together the egg and buttermilk.

Heat the oil in a frying pan over medium-high. Dip the fish in the buttermilk mixture and then in the flour mixture. Place it in the hot oil. Fry the fish for about 4 minutes on each side until the coating is golden brown. Serve hot.

# Tennessee Trout

Chef Matt Bolus has fished all over the Southeast. He still remembers his first fishing trip in Florida with his father, and he later learned to fly-fish in the mountain streams of East Tennessee where he grew up. Then after a stint on the coast in Charleston, he moved to Nashville. He's known for his superb cooking—and fish dishes. This simple trout dish is the type he makes at home for family.

**Makes 4 servings**

4   trout, cleaned, heads removed, ribs and spine cut out

    Kosher salt and freshly ground black pepper

¼   cup (60 ml) grapeseed oil

4   tablespoons (55 g) butter, cut into 1 tablespoon pieces

8   sprigs thyme

1   lemon, cut in half, seeds removed

Place the trout on paper towels skin side down, and open them up so the flesh is facing up. Pat the flesh dry with paper towels. Season the flesh with salt and pepper. Close the fish back together.

In a pan large enough to cook two fish at a time, heat half the oil over medium-high. You will know the oil is hot enough to cook in when you see ripples in the pan and light wisps of smoke.

Season the skin side of two of the fish with salt and pepper. Place the fish in the pan. You should hear a sizzling noise when the fish hit the pan. Cook the fish for roughly 4 minutes or until the skin is golden and crisp. Using a spatula (a fish spatula if you have one), gently turn the fish over, being careful not to tear the skin. Cook the fish on this side for 2 minutes longer, then add 2 tablespoons of butter and 4 sprigs of the thyme to the pan. Allow the butter to completely melt and start to foam up.

Squeeze one of the lemon halves over the fish and, using a spoon, baste the fish with the butter for another 2 minutes. If needed, you can carefully open the fish to see if they are cooked to your liking. Wipe out the pan and repeat the above steps with the remaining ingredients.

# Smoked Trout and Turnip Green Dip

## *with* Hot Sauce

This recipe essentially combines spinach dip—but with heartier turnip greens—with a smoked trout dip held together by cream cheese and sour cream. Add a sleeve of saltines and a bottle of hot sauce, and you have a hit.

**Makes enough dip for 10 to 12 people**

- 2 tablespoons olive oil
- 1 onion, diced
- 2 tablespoons garlic, finely chopped
- 8 ounces (225 g) turnip greens, cooked and drained
- ¼ teaspoon sea salt
- ¼ teaspoon black pepper
- 1 (8-ounce/225-g) package cream cheese, softened
- ¾ cup (180 ml) sour cream
- 4 shakes Worcestershire sauce
- ½ cup (55 g) chopped pecans
- Juice of ½ lemon
- ½ pound (225 g) smoked trout
- 2 tablespoons grated Parmesan
- Saltines for serving
- Cayenne hot sauce for serving

Preheat the oven to 400°F (205°C).

In a medium sauté pan, heat the oil over medium and sauté the onion and garlic until they are soft, about 8 minutes. Add the turnip greens and sauté for another 3 minutes, stirring. Season with the salt and pepper. Allow the mixture to cool.

In a medium bowl, cream together the cream cheese and sour cream. Add the Worcestershire, pecans, and lemon juice. Stir in the trout and add the onion and spinach mixture, stirring to combine.

Lightly grease a deep pie plate or square baking dish. Pour the mixture into the dish and top it with the Parmesan. Bake the dip for 20 minutes. Serve it hot, with crackers and a bottle of hot sauce.

# Fried Crappie
## *with* Hushpuppies

3 cups (365 g) cornmeal

2 cups (365 g) all-purpose flour

¼ teaspoon black pepper

¼ teaspoon lemon pepper

¼ teaspoon dried thyme

2 cups (480 ml) buttermilk

Vegetable oil for frying

4 crappie fillets

Hushpuppies for serving (recipe follows)

Crappie (pronounced like croppie) has been called one of the best-tasting freshwater catches found in lakes in this region. It's a popular game fish from the sunfish family and one that casual weekend fishermen also enjoy for sport and for its mild, sweet taste. Middle Tennessee home cook Barbara Gourley Davenport and her husband have been making this simple pan-fried version for about forty years. (The pair went fishing on their second date, after all.)

If you would like to use the same oil for both the hushpuppies and fish, then begin by making the hushpuppies. You will need to add additional oil after frying the bread. Then keep the hushpuppies warm while frying the fish.

**Makes 4 servings**

In a paper bag, combine the cornmeal, flour, both peppers, and thyme.

Pour the buttermilk into a shallow bowl.

Pour enough oil into a deep skillet to fill it to a depth of about 2 inches (5 cm). Heat the oil to 375°F (190°C).

Meanwhile (taking care to keep your eye on the heating oil), dip the fish fillets into the buttermilk, coating all sides. Drop them into the bag with the dry ingredients and shake to coat them completely.

Slide the fish into the hot oil and fry the fillets until they are golden brown and floating, about 5 minutes on each side. Transfer them to a paper-towel-lined plate. Serve them with the hushpuppies.

## Hushpuppies

**Makes about 30 hushpuppies**

3 cups (415 g) self-rising cornmeal

½ cup (60 g) self-rising flour

2 large eggs

1½ cups (360 ml) buttermilk

1 teaspoon black pepper

1 cup (120 g) finely chopped onion

Vegetable oil for frying

In a medium bowl, combine the cornmeal, flour, eggs, buttermilk, pepper, and onion.

Pour about 1½ inches (3.8 cm) oil into a deep skillet and heat it to 350°F (175°C). Drop walnut-size spoonfuls of batter into the hot oil. Be careful not to overcrowd the pan. Fry them, turning them occasionally, for 3 to 4 minutes, until they are crisp and dark golden brown. Transfer them to a paper-towel-lined plate to drain while you cook the remaining batches of hushpuppies.

# Nashville Hot Fish

Inspiration for this dish comes from Bolton's Spicy Chicken & Fish. Lightly season the cornmeal for dredging the fish, then add the wet and dry spices after frying to allow for customization of heat.

**Makes 4 servings**

- 4 mild white fish fillets
- Sea salt and black pepper
- 2 cups (245 g) yellow cornmeal
- ½ teaspoon paprika
- 2 tablespoons plus 1 teaspoon cayenne pepper
- 1 tablespoon chili powder
- ¼ teaspoon ground cumin
- 2 tablespoons ketchup
- 2 tablespoons hot sauce
- 2 cups (480 ml) vegetable oil
- 4 slices white bread
- Yellow mustard
- Pickles
- 1 large white onion, sliced

Place the fish on a clean surface. Gently pat it dry and season it with salt and pepper. Allow the fish to come up to room temperature.

In a shallow dish, combine the cornmeal with the paprika and 1 teaspoon of the cayenne.

In a small bowl prepare the dry spice by combining the remaining 2 tablespoons cayenne with the chili powder, cumin, and ¼ teaspoon salt.

In another small bowl, combine the ketchup and hot sauce.

In a 9-inch (23-cm) cast-iron skillet, heat the oil over medium-high until it reaches 325 to 350°F (165 to 175°C). Dredge the fish in the cornmeal mixture. When the oil has reached the proper temperature, carefully place the fish into it using tongs. Be careful not to overcrowd the fish. Fry the fillets for 2 to 3 minutes per side, depending on their thickness. When they are golden and lightly browned, transfer them to a paper-towel-lined plate.

While the fish is still warm, sprinkle it with the desired amount of dry spice to get the heat you want.

When the fish has cooled enough to serve, place each piece on a slice of white bread and stripe it with yellow mustard and the ketchup mixture, then pile on pickles and white onion.

# Catfish Tacos

*with* Charred Corn, Peppers, *and* Lemon Aioli

Bailey Spaulding, brewmaster and cofounder of Jackalope Brewing Company, and her fiancé, chef Luke Williams, often cook together at home to make dishes like this one. Pair Luke's recipe for tacos with Bailey's Jackalope Bearwalker, a maple brown ale.

**Makes 4 to 8 servings**

*For the fish tacos:*

- 2 pounds (910 g) catfish fillets, cut into strips 1 inch (2.5 cm) wide

  Kosher salt and black pepper

- 2 cups (245 g) cornmeal

- 2 cups (480 ml) grapeseed oil

*For serving:*

- 16 (6-inch/15-cm) corn tortillas

*For the charred corn:*

- 4 ears corn, shucked

  Grapeseed oil

  Kosher salt and black pepper

*For the salsa:*

- 5 banana peppers, chopped into medium dice

- 1 white onion, chopped into medium dice

- 1 red or green jalapeño, chopped into small dice

- 2 cloves garlic, minced

- ½ tablespoon ground cumin

- 1 teaspoon hot sauce, or more if desired

  Kosher salt and black pepper

*For the lemon aioli:*

- 2 large egg yolks

- 1 cup (240 ml) grapeseed oil

- 3 tablespoons lemon juice

  Zest of 1 large lemon

  Kosher salt and black pepper

*Prepare the fish tacos:*
Preheat the oven to 300°F (150°C).

Place the fish strips on a clean plate or cookie sheet. Season them generously with salt and pepper—we are not seasoning the cornmeal, so this allows for even seasoning of each piece of fish.

In a large bowl, toss a few pieces of fish at a time with the cornmeal to coat them thoroughly. Repeat until all the fish is coated.

In a large cast-iron skillet, heat the oil on medium-high until it is hot, but not smoking—somewhere around 325 to 350°F (165 to 175°C).

Once the oil has reached this temperature, carefully place your strips of catfish into the pan and allow them to cook till they are golden brown, 2 to 3 minutes on each side. Transfer them to a paper-towel-lined plate as they are done.

Wrap your tortillas in aluminum foil and place them in the oven for 7 to 10 minutes to warm.

*Prepare the charred corn:*
To char the corn, you can use either a grill or a hot skillet. For the grill, lightly coat the ears of corn in oil, salt, and pepper and char them over a hot grill until the kernels are beginning to blacken, but be careful not to let them burn.

If you're using a skillet, cut the corn off the cob and toss it with salt and pepper. Add ¼ inch (6 mm) oil to the skillet and put it over high heat. When the oil just begins to smoke, add the corn and sauté until the kernels begin to color, taking care not to burn them.

*Prepare the salsa:*
In a medium bowl, combine all the salsa ingredients. Taste and add more salt, pepper, or hot sauce to your preference.

*Prepare the lemon aioli:*
In a blender or food processor or with an electric hand mixer, blend together the yolks. As the machine runs, slowly drizzle in the oil until combined. Then drizzle in your lemon juice and zest until smooth. Taste and season with salt, pepper, or lemon juice if needed.

To assemble the tacos, top two warmed tortillas with two pieces of fish down the middle. Add some salsa and charred corn. Finish with the lemon aioli. Repeat with the remaining ingredients.

# Barbecue Shrimp

Barbecue shrimp is no doubt a New Orleans dish—leave the heads on, throw in more butter than ought to be right, add a bit of Creole seasoning. So to make this dish a bit more Nashville, it's cooked in packets on the grill with a kick of cayenne instead. Heads off, but the butter stays.

**Makes 4 appetizer servings**

¼  cup (60 ml) Worcestershire sauce

¼  teaspoon cayenne pepper

3  cloves garlic, minced

2  lemons, juiced and thinly sliced into rounds

1  cup (2 sticks/225 g) butter

16  large shrimp, with tails but peeled, deveined, and heads removed

**Baguette for serving**

Preheat a charcoal or gas grill to high.

In a medium saucepan over medium heat, combine the Worcestershire sauce, cayenne, garlic, and lemon juice. Once the mixture is warm, begin adding the butter, about 1 tablespoon at a time, whisking constantly until it is combined.

Tear or cut aluminum foil into eight neat squares about 8 inches (20 cm) to a side. Arrange them in four stacks of two squares each. Place four shrimp on each doubled piece of foil and shape the foil into a little bowl. Divide the lemon slices among the packets as well. Pour about ¼ cup (60 ml) of sauce into each shrimp packet. Fold the foil up tightly and place the packets on the heated grill. Grill the packets for about 8 minutes.

Serve the shrimp with the remaining sauce on the side and baguette for sopping.

# Fish and Grits

While shrimp and grits have a traditional place on Low Country tables, you're more apt to find a seasoned white fish over grits in this region.

**Makes 4 servings**

## For the blackened fish:

- 1 tablespoon paprika
- 1 tablespoon garlic powder
- 1 tablespoon dried thyme
- 1 tablespoon dried oregano
- 1 teaspoon chili powder
- 1 teaspoon cayenne pepper
- 1 teaspoon kosher salt
- 1 teaspoon black pepper
- 2 tablespoons grapeseed oil
- 4 whiting fillets (or catfish or tilapia)

## For the grits:

- 1 teaspoon salt
- 2 cups (340 g) grits (not quick-cut)
- 2 tablespoons unsalted butter
- ⅓ cup (80 ml) half-and-half
- 1 teaspoon black pepper

*Prepare the fish:*
In a shallow dish, combine the paprika, garlic powder, thyme, oregano, chili powder, cayenne, salt, and pepper.

In a medium skillet, heat the oil over medium-high. Coat the fillets in the blackening seasoning and place them in the hot pan. Depending on the size of your skillet, fry the fish in batches so as not to overcrowd them, for 2 to 3 minutes per side, until the fish is flaky and white. Transfer them to a paper-towel-lined plate as they are done.

*Prepare the grits:*
In a medium saucepan, bring 6 cups (1.4 L) water to a boil. Add the salt. Add the grits, stirring, and bring the mixture to a simmer over low. Cover and continue to simmer for 20 to 30 minutes, stirring regularly. Remove the pan from the heat, then stir in the butter and half-and-half. Serve the fish over the grits.

# Grilled Freshwater Bass

My father, an avid fisherman, taught me this recipe for freshwater bass. Though he often fishes for trout in streams and rivers, he learned to make this dish in college when he fished with friends in the nearby lakes.

**Makes 4 servings**

½  cup (1 stick/115 g) butter, plus more for pan and grilling

1  tablespoon kosher salt

1  tablespoon hickory smoked salt

4  freshwater bass fillets

⅓  cup (80 ml) lemon juice

1  teaspoon dried sweet basil

6  paper-thin slices lemon

6  sprigs Italian parsley

Preheat a charcoal grill. Lightly butter a grill-safe baking pan.

In a small bowl, combine the kosher and hickory salts. Use a little of this mixture to salt the fillets.

In a small saucepan, melt ½ cup (1 stick/115 g) butter over medium heat. Add the lemon juice, then rub the basil in your hands and add it to the sauce.

Place the fillets on the prepared pan and pour lemon sauce over them. Arrange the lemon slices on top of the fish. Top with the parsley.

Place the pan on the hot grill. Drop a couple pats of butter onto the hot coals to create more smoke. Close the grill and smoke the fish for 5 minutes or until it is flaky. Serve it warm.

# THE RECIPES

———

# VEGGIES + SIDES

**W**hen the air turns crisp in October, a visit to the outdoor sheds at the Nashville Farmers' Market has shoppers clutching cups of coffee and winding between towers of pumpkins and baskets of shiny eggplant, dried peppers, and beans. Fresh apple-cinnamon doughnuts perfume the air as vendors pass around samples of blackberry jams and chunky salsas, and Amish bakers stand proudly behind rows of caramel cakes, pecan pies, and loaves of salt-rising bread.

And there among the last of the season's tomatoes and yellow squash and baskets brimming with turnip greens, you could spot Troy Smiley of Smiley's Farm dressed in a long denim duster jacket with a lip full of tobacco. A fifth-generation farmer, Troy remembers coming to the market at age five with his father.

Over the years, the Smileys raised "a little bit of everything" including fifteen acres of strawberries until the 1980s. But these days, they're mostly known for their vegetables.

Tennesseans love their farm-fresh vegetables, from green beans cooked down with a spoonful of bacon drippings to others prepared minimally, such as slices of deep red tomato with just a sprinkle of salt.

In homes across Nashville, you'll find the seasons represented as both the main course and side dishes, but you'll also find them on daily menus at plate-lunch restaurants. Meat-and-three restaurants offer customers a choice of one meat from a daily selection such as fried chicken or roast beef and three vegetable sides like okra, turnip greens, or stewed tomatoes. But one look down the steam table line at these establishments proves the name a bit misleading. "Meat-and-seventeen-or-twenty" would be more accurate.

In this section we celebrate those vegetables and growers like Troy. The recipes include traditional yet fresh ways of preparing our harvests from backyard gardens and from the country farms just a few minutes' drive from downtown Nashville. These stories and recipes evoke the sounds of lively conversations between aunts and grandmothers snapping green beans over the pot and the spirit of impromptu gatherings called just because, on the way back home, someone picked up a watermelon to share.

## KITCHEN PLAYLIST

These songs celebrate vegetables and side dishes, as well as the hard work of the farmers who grow them.

**Farmer's Blues**
MARTY STUART

This song laments the hard life of a farmer. Stuart, a Mississippi native, played on *Hee Haw* at age fourteen. He eventually joined Johnny Cash's band before he headed out on his own to pursue a solo career.

**Country Gentleman**
CHET ATKINS

The legendary guitar player credited with creating the Nashville sound had an unofficial daily table at his favorite meat-and-three called Hap Townes.

**Play It Loud, Ray**
JACOB JONES

In this tune, Jones sings about margaritas, fried chicken, and greens.

**Meat and Three**
HIGHWATER

Nashville-based funk band sings about chess pie, sweet iced tea, fried chicken, mashed potatoes, and collard greens.

# Nashville's Meat-and-Threes

Where Nashville sets a welcome table.

When Alisa Martin stood in line for the steam table lunch at Arnold's Country Kitchen, she joked with her friend and owner Kahlil Arnold about an old photo they'd seen for the "Dolly Parton Diet" involving fried chicken and mashed potatoes.

The stranger behind her overheard and confirmed that the diet is for real. Not because she had tried it, necessarily, but because she was there that day to pick up Dolly's to-go lunch.

You never know who might stand in line at Arnold's. Nashville food writer John Egerton called the line that leads to a stack of red trays the great equalizer. Judges and music produc-

ers wait for slabs of meat loaf, scoops of turnip greens, and side plates of sliced tomatoes and corncakes just like the postman and John Prine. It's Nashville's kitchen table.

And regardless who you wait with, the line will likely stretch out the front door of the shotgun space between the gravy brown walls plastered in newspaper clippings, signed black-and-white headshots of singers like Brenda Lee, and the restaurant's framed James Beard America's Classics medal. Kahlil Arnold might spoon gravy into your mashed potatoes, flash a flirty smile, and urge you to try the green beans while slipping you a slice of peach pie. His younger brother, Franz, carves the roast beef as his older brother, Lon, refills containers of candied yams from the kitchen. Their mother, Rose, heads up the line at the cash register, where she'll hand you a Styrofoam cup of iced tea.

While Arnold's isn't the only meat-and-three in town, it's definitely one of the most famous. From Sylvan Park and Swett's to the Pie Wagon, the Silver Sands, and the bygone Hap Townes restaurant, some say Nashville has more meat-and-threes than other Southern cities. At Hap Townes restaurant, Chet Atkins had a favorite table and Shel Silverstein would often call the moment he arrived in town to hear the menu. He would beg Hap to stay open until he could get down to pick up a plate, and Hap always would.

No one's been able to pinpoint the exact reason Nashville loves its meat-and-threes, though Kahlil Arnold supposes they sprang from the farm living that happened on the edges of town. Cooks made the most of what they had just as you would on a farm. You used every part of the animals and incorporated harvested vegetables in various ways.

Even today, if Kahlil has leftover fried chicken, it might go into the chicken and dumplings. The remainder of the creamed corn might stretch to make—and flavor—a corn pudding. The restaurant only opens during the week, a holdover from the days when downtown Nashville once looked like a ghost town on weekends as workers fled back to the country or suburbs.

Kahlil's father, Jack, who started Arnold's Country Kitchen in the early 1980s, understands farm cooking, having grown up on one.

Kahlil began washing pots at the restaurant at age thirteen. He left the family business in his twenties to work at another institution, the Loveless Cafe. And though he was on track to become a manager there, he returned to Arnold's at age twenty-eight when his father began to show signs of aging. The restaurant has since thrived under his leadership.

Tandy Wilson, respected chef of City House, says he makes a point of taking visitors not only to Arnold's, but also to the Silver Sands Soul Food, where you'll find buttery bowls of chicken and dumplings, crisp fried catfish, white beans, greens, and pork neck bones.

Owner Sophia Vaughn takes orders—and takes temperatures on the day. Having a bad one? She might offer you one of the BC headache powders that she keeps behind the line for guests along with a piece of hot water cornbread and a fried chicken thigh. Sophia took over the business from her mother and aunt, who owned the restaurant for more than fifty years. She arrives at three o'clock every morning to begin cooking the breakfast, and she wraps up her workday by taking a plate of food to a regular customer who can no longer drive.

Not everybody has family here, she says, but the meat-and-threes of Nashville serve the home cooked meals that can make people feel as if they do.

Kahlil Arnold carries on a Nashville meat-and-three tradition with the business his father Jack started more than thirty years ago.

The Arnold family has served many famous regulars, like the late Porter Wagoner. But Nashvillians and visitors of all backgrounds have a seat at their tables.

# Squash Casserole

More attractive than the versions I grew up with, which had a blanket of crispy French onions over canned soup, this casserole has layers of colors and flavors. It's an homage to Arnold's Country Kitchen, where squash casserole is a favorite. This version has a base of sour cream, white cheddar, and a touch of mayonnaise bubbling up into squash scattered with ribbons of pimiento. Then comes a rich row of deeply caramelized onions and a crispy dusting of buttered bread crumbs and parsley.

**Makes about 8 servings**

| | |
|---|---|
| 2½ | tablespoons butter, plus more for pan |
| 3 | onions, halved and thinly sliced |
| ¼ | cup (60 ml) balsamic vinegar |
| 1¼ | teaspoons sea salt |
| 1 | tablespoon extra-virgin olive oil |
| 7 | medium yellow squash, sliced |
| ¾ | cup (180 ml) sour cream |
| ¼ | cup (60 ml) mayonnaise |
| 1 | cup (120 g) shredded sharp white cheddar cheese |
| 3 | tablespoons prepared plain bread crumbs |
| 2 | tablespoons chopped fresh parsley |
| 1 | (4-ounce/113-g) jar of sliced pimientos, drained |

Preheat the oven to 350°F (175°C) and butter a baking dish.

In a large skillet, melt 1½ tablespoons of the butter over medium-high. Add the onions. They'll begin to soften after about 10 minutes, and after about 20 minutes, you might need to turn down the heat. Continue cooking them for 40 minutes to an hour, until they are brown. Add the vinegar and stir to scrape up any dark bits on the bottom of the pan. Season with ¼ teaspoon of the salt. Set the onions aside.

In another large skillet, heat the oil over medium-high, then sauté the squash until it is beginning to soften but not yet losing its shape. Season it with 1 teaspoon salt. Set the squash aside.

In a small bowl, combine the sour cream, mayonnaise, and cheese. Melt the remaining 1 tablespoon butter and pour it into a second small bowl; stir in the bread crumbs and parsley.

Assemble the casserole by layering the sour cream mixture on the bottom of the prepared dish, then the squash, then a scattering of pimientos, then caramelized onions and the bread crumb mixture. Bake for 25 to 30 minutes or until the casserole is hot and bubbly. Allow it to cool for 10 to 15 minutes to make it easier to slice and serve.

# Tomato Pie

I have seen—and loved—tomato pies made with spoonfuls of mayonnaise, cheddar cheese, and Ritz crackers crumbled on top. I'm certainly not going to disparage those buttery Ritz jewels. My mother and I would often work our way down a wax-paper sleeve of them with a Coke, our version of taking afternoon tea.

Still, I'd rather crackers not cover up the wrinkled, roasted beauty of the tomatoes in this pie. I also like mixing tomato types and sizes to create a palette of colors on top. And with pieces of bacon, a little mayonnaise (but not too much), and basil leaves, it's like an amped up BLT wrapped in the charm of pie.

**Makes 1 pie**

2 pounds (910 g) medium-size tomatoes in various colors

½ teaspoon fine kosher salt

½ cup (120 ml) mayonnaise

½ cup (60 g) shredded sharp white cheddar cheese

¼ cup (30 g) grated Parmesan

1 (9-inch/23-cm) piecrust, store-bought or homemade

¼ teaspoon freshly ground black pepper

5 to 6 slices thick-cut bacon, fried crisp and broken into small pieces

10 basil leaves

Handful of cherry tomatoes in various colors

4 thyme sprigs

Slice the large tomatoes into rounds ¼ inch (6 mm) thick and place them on paper towels. Let them sit for about 10 minutes, then flip them over onto fresh paper towels and sprinkle them with the salt. Let them sit about 10 minutes more. You don't want them to be too juicy before baking, because that could make your pie soupy.

Preheat the oven to 400°F (205°C).

Prepare the filling by combining the mayonnaise, cheddar, and Parmesan.

Arrange a layer of tomatoes in the bottom of the piecrust. Sprinkle on the pepper and half of the bacon, then layer on five of the basil leaves and spread half of the mayonnaise mixture over the basil. Repeat, ending with a final layer of sliced tomatoes, placed so that you can fit the cherry tomatoes on top as well. Scatter the thyme sprigs across the top of the pie.

Bake the pie for about 30 minutes, then fold strips of aluminum foil around the rim of the pie to keep the edges from turning too brown and continue baking for another 15 minutes. Allow the pie to cool before serving.

# Skillet Corn and Zucchini

"Fried corn," which sounds more decadent than it probably needs to, usually just means sweet fresh corn pan-fried in butter or bacon drippings. I also like tossing in a couple of zucchini and some thyme because these flavors go (and grow) so naturally together in the summer season.

**Makes about 6 servings**

- 4 ears fresh corn, husk and silk removed
- 2 tablespoons butter
- ½ onion, finely diced
- 2 cloves garlic, minced
- ¼ teaspoon kosher salt
- ¼ teaspoon black pepper
- 1 tablespoon fresh thyme
- 2 medium zucchini, sliced lengthwise and cut into half-moons

Cut the corn off the cob. I like cutting into a pie plate because it's shallow enough to work in and the edges keep the kernels from bouncing out.

Heat the butter in a skillet over medium-high until it is melted and hot. Add the onion and cook until softened. Then add the garlic and cook for 1 minute. Add the salt, pepper, thyme, zucchini, and corn, cooking over medium until the zucchini is tender and the corn is starting to brown in a few places, about 10 minutes. Serve warm or at room temperature.

# Fried Green Tomatoes

Of course there's more than one way to fry a tomato—dipped into egg or buttermilk and then maybe dusted with panko or flour. But really all you need is salt, pepper, flour, and a touch of cornmeal for texture.

While you can serve these tomatoes on their own, Chef Hal Holden-Bache at Lockeland Table in East Nashville occasionally dresses them up with a dab of hot pepper jelly and serves them alongside a crisp, cool wedge salad topped with blue cheese and a few crumbles of bacon.

**Makes 4 servings**

2  green tomatoes

Sea salt and black pepper

¾  cup (95 g) all-purpose flour

½  cup (60 g) yellow cornmeal

Vegetable oil for frying

Slice the tomatoes about ¼ inch (6 mm) thick. Season both sides with salt and pepper

In a shallow bowl, combine the flour and cornmeal. Add an additional ½ teaspoon salt.

Pour about ¼ inch (6 mm) of oil into the skillet and heat it to 350°F (175°C). Cook the tomato slices for 2 minutes on each side or until they're golden all over and brown in some places. Drain them on paper towels and serve warm.

# Stewed Tomatoes

Simple tomatoes stretch to make a hearty warm meal in this old-time recipe. Though it's incredibly easy, it was a favorite at Hap Townes meat-and-three restaurant. I've heard of adding leftover biscuits or even macaroni, but the most common way to add heft to this dish is to use a couple pieces of toasted white bread.

**Makes about 6 servings**

1  (28-ounce/794-g) can whole tomatoes

4  tablespoons (55 g) butter

1  tablespoon granulated sugar

½  teaspoon sea salt

½  teaspoon black pepper

2  to 3 slices toasted bread

In a medium saucepan, combine the tomatoes and their juices, butter, sugar, salt, and pepper. Bring to a boil over medium heat. Reduce the heat to medium-low and simmer for 10 minutes. During the last 5 minutes of cooking, tear the bread into pieces and drop it into the tomato mixture. Stir to combine and serve warm.

**Fried Green Tomatoes**

# Stewed Raisins

Hap Townes spooned out this decadent side dish at his legendary Nashville meat-and-three. Sort of like a Southern chutney or the buttery-tart filling of a pie, a spoonful goes a long way alongside savory meats and vegetables. The ingredients are basic, but the end result is an indulgence. Though Hap often used dark raisins, I prefer golden raisins and omitted some of the sugar often seen in traditional recipes.

**Makes 6 to 8 side-dish servings**

1  (15-ounce/425-g) box golden raisins

2  tablespoons butter

2  tablespoons all-purpose flour

2  tablespoons lemon juice

In a medium saucepan, cover the raisins with water. Bring them to a boil and then reduce the heat to a simmer. Cook the water down until it's just below the raisins, about 15 minutes. Add the butter and stir until it melts, then stir in the flour to thicken the mixture. Add the lemon juice and serve.

# Spicy Honeyed Greens

These greens have sweet heat and a hint of pork flavor. If you're making these for New Year's, substitute a ham hock left over from Christmas dinner for the bacon.

**Makes about 6 servings**

2  large bunches greens (I prefer collards)

2  slices thick-cut bacon, cut into ¼-inch (6-mm) strips

1  yellow onion, sliced

¾  to 1 teaspoon crushed red pepper flakes, depending on how spicy you like your greens

1  teaspoon kosher salt

2  cups (480 ml) chicken stock

2  tablespoons cider vinegar

Honey to taste (I like about 1½ tablespoons)

Remove the stems from the greens, fold the leaves over, and slice them diagonally into pieces about 1 inch (2.5 cm) wide. Place them in a large bowl of water to wash. Drain them in colander and repeat if they still feel gritty.

Heat a stockpot over medium-high and fry the bacon until it is starting to brown. Add the onion and cook over medium until it browns, about 10 minutes.

Add the red pepper flakes and salt and cook 1 minute more, stirring. Then pour in the stock and begin adding the greens in batches, waiting until they wilt before adding the next batch. Add the vinegar and enough water to just cover the greens. Add the honey (begin with 1 tablespoon of honey and add more during the cooking process as you taste it). Bring the mixture to a boil, then immediately reduce the heat to simmer it, stirring occasionally, for about an hour. Taste and adjust the seasonings to your liking before serving.

# Cornmeal Fried Okra

## *with* Sriracha-Buttermilk Dipping Sauce

Frying okra, as my mother says, can help cook the slimy parts out—or mostly, anyway. But she doesn't deep-fry okra, as you'll find it in many restaurants; that causes little cocoons to form about the okra, leaving it mostly just cooked, with the gooey insides intact.

In this version, the flour-cornmeal mixture becomes part of the vegetable and its flavor. The addition of a green tomato also adds a tart kick that brightens the dish among the musty, earthy flavor of okra.

**Makes about 4 servings**

1   **pound (455 g) okra**

1   **green tomato**

¼   **teaspoon kosher salt**

⅛   **teaspoon black pepper**

¼   **cup (60 ml) vegetable oil, or more if needed**

1   **cup (125 g) all-purpose flour**

¼   **cup (40 g) yellow cornmeal**

    **Sriracha-Buttermilk Dipping Sauce for serving (recipe follows)**

Wash the okra and place it in a bowl. Wash the tomato and cut it into ¼-inch (6-mm) cubes, and place them in the bowl with the okra. Season the mixture with salt and pepper and toss.

Heat the oil over high. In a shallow bowl, combine the flour and cornmeal. Quickly dredge the okra and tomato in the flour mixture. Shake off the excess and drop them into the hot pan. Depending on the size of your pan, you might want to work in batches—you don't want to crowd the okra. Fry it for about

1 minute, then reduce the heat to medium or medium-high. Continue to fry, turning it occasionally with a spatula, for 15 to 20 minutes or until it is well done and dark in some places. You might need to add more oil if the pan starts to get too dry.

Remove the okra and tomatoes from the pan with a slotted spoon or spatula and place them on a paper-towel-lined plate to cool and drain. Serve with Sriracha-Buttermilk Dipping Sauce.

## Sriracha-Buttermilk Dipping Sauce

Makes a little more than ¼ cup (60 ml)

¼   **cup (60 ml) buttermilk**

3   **tablespoons mayonnaise**

1   **tablespoon Sriracha**

In a small bowl, whisk together the buttermilk and mayonnaise, and then whisk in the Sriracha. Serve with the fried okra for dipping.

# Roasted Okra

Many Southerners like me grow up knowing okra only fried or bobbing in soup. So I'm thankful to the folks at Bells Bend Farms for teaching me this version several years ago. They used purple okra plucked from their property and prepared it simply—roasted with olive oil.

**Makes about 4 servings**

1 pound (455 g) okra

1 tablespoon extra-virgin olive oil

3 pinches kosher salt

Freshly ground black pepper

Preheat the oven to 450°F (230°C). Line a baking sheet with aluminum foil.

Wash the okra and dry it on a towel. Trim and discard the tough ends and slice it lengthwise. In a large bowl, toss the okra with the olive oil and salt. Then spread it in a single layer on the prepared baking sheet.

Roast the okra for about 10 minutes. Turn it with a spatula and roast it 5 minutes more. Sprinkle it with pepper and serve warm.

# Collard Rolls

The Keys Motel isn't the type of place that draws lots of tourists. For many, it's a transitional spot between the streets and a permanent residence where making the $650 monthly rent can come with a lot of unknowns.

Yet Johnnie Falls has lived in the hotel for more than four years, and a constant she discovered just around the corner is the community meal at Trinity United Methodist Church. The weekly dinner served family-style by the Nashville Food Project might include a lentil shepherd's pie fluffy with sweet potato topping or collard green rolls bulging with beef and rice and smothered in tomato sauce. Ingredients in these home-cooked meals come from Nashville Food Project's gardens or are gleaned from other farms and markets.

Beyond the food, it's a place where Johnnie can check on her friend "Pops," a homeless man she helped get into rehab, or to just sit a minute and talk in a safe place.

Then when Johnnie goes home to the motel, she takes off her white sticker nametag written in marker and she saves it.

"I have a notebook with my name on it," she said. "I put every one of my name tags in it."

Eating fresh food is important for health, but eating it in the company of others also matters, as isolation has been named one of the most tragic consequences of poverty. That's part of why the Nashville Food Project, which isn't officially affiliated with any religious groups, has evolved over its years to not only feed community but to help create it. All the while, the group does good with the generosity of the city as well as the resourcefulness and talents of home cooks who help create, prepare, and serve about one thousand hot meals per week. Even more remarkable, the meals—creatively pieced together with food grown, gleaned, and donated from places like Whole Foods, Second Harvest Food Bank, and Chipotle—cost just around 25 cents per meal.

When the Nashville Food Project began in 2007, the group served sandwiches made with cold cuts and handed out paper sacks with fruit and bottled water. The organization sometimes gave away produce from farms as donations but soon realized that some recipients either didn't know what to do with yellow squash, for example, or didn't have the means to prepare it. So the project evolved to serve hot meals from trucks made out of grown and gleaned produce and donations.

The project also planted a garden in 2010. Then, after a few years of driving meals to the hotels and apartment complexes of those in need, the project evolved, and organizers began looking for ways to serve meals in an environment that brings people together to eat and take time to socialize and connect.

**For the filling:**

2 tablespoons olive oil

1 small onion, chopped

1 tablespoon garlic, minced

2 cups (240 g) cooked rice

2 cups (300 g) cooked ground beef

⅓ cup (55 g) raisins or dried cranberries

**For the sauce:**

1 tablespoon olive oil

1 small onion, chopped

1 tablespoon garlic

2 pounds (910 g) fresh tomatoes, diced, or 1 (28-ounce/794-g) can crushed tomatoes

3 ounces (85 g) tomato paste

1 teaspoon paprika

½ teaspoon ground cinnamon

1½ to 2 teaspoons light brown sugar

1 tablespoon cider vinegar

Kosher salt and black pepper

**For the collards:**

2 bunches collards, cleaned

1 tablespoon salt

"Having the food support any community effort," says outreach manager Grace Biggs, "that's what our eye is toward now."

This recipe comes from meals manager Anne Sale and Ann Fundis, volunteer for the Nashville Food Project and enthusiastic home cook. By using collards in place of cabbage, they give the Hungarian-flavored dish a Southern feel. Cider vinegar and raisins add tang and balance out the bitterness of the collards.

**Makes 18 to 20 servings**

*Prepare the filling:*
Heat the oil in a large skillet. Add the onion and sauté until it is beginning to soften, about 3 minutes. Add the garlic and cook for a minute longer before adding the rice, beef, and raisins. Continue to cook on medium-low, breaking up the beef with a spatula, until the mixture is combined and warmed through.

*Prepare the sauce:*
Heat the oil in a large skillet. Add the onion and sauté until it is beginning to soften, about 3 minutes. Add the garlic and cook for a minute longer. Add the tomatoes, tomato paste, paprika, cinnamon, brown sugar, and vinegar. Taste and adjust seasoning with salt and pepper.

*Prepare the collards:*
Place the collards in a large stockpot and cover them with water. Add the salt. Bring the water to a boil and continue boiling for 10 minutes until the greens are soft.

Preheat the oven to 350°F (175°C).

*Assemble the rolls:*
Lay out a collard leaf on a cutting board and trim the thick stem to make it flat. Place a couple of heaping spoonfuls of the stuffing on the leaf and roll it up burrito-style by bringing left and right sides in first, followed by the top and bottom edges. Place the filled roll seam side down in a casserole dish. Repeat with the remaining collard leaves and filling.

Spoon the sauce over the collard rolls. Bake them for about 45 minutes. Serve warm.

Anne Sale started working at the
Nashville Food Project as a volunteer.

Now as meals manager, Anne helps put together creative hot meals with donated, grown, and gleaned ingredients.

# New Year's Day Black-Eyed Peas

In 2001, Chef Margot McCormack had just opened her Margot Café and Bar, a French-inspired spot in a gritty East Nashville community. She had returned to her native Nashville from New York, where she'd had access to the greenmarkets of the city and the fertile Hudson Valley while attending the Culinary Institute of America. But coming home, she wondered, "Where are all the Tennessee farmers?"

Then along came Tana Comer, an organic grower with a basket of produce. She dropped it off for Margot and left. Since then, the relationship between farmer and chef has blossomed. With the help of vendors like Tana, Margot ushered in a food movement and became someone *TIME* magazine would eventually call the Alice Waters of Nashville.

As for Tana, the vegetarian forgoes the pork fat added to many Southern black-eyed peas and greens recipes on New Year's Day. Her version is healthful but flavorful, and she serves it with a side of kale and skillet cornbread. A cayenne hot sauce tops off the meal.

**Makes 4 to 6 servings**

1½  cups (245 g) dried black-eyed peas

2  tablespoons canola oil

½  cup (60 g) chopped yellow onion

2  celery stalks with their leaves, chopped

6  cups (1.4 L) vegetable broth

Kosher salt and black pepper

½  cup (90 g) sprouted basmati rice

Cornbread, for serving

Cayenne hot sauce, for serving

Place the black-eyed peas in a bowl or pot and add enough water to cover them by about 2 inches (5 cm). Soak them for 8 hours.

In a saucepan, heat the oil and cook the onion and celery for a couple of minutes until they begin softening. Add the broth and bring the liquid to a boil. Drain the black-eyed peas and add them to the broth mixture. Reduce the heat to a simmer and cook the mixture until the peas are tender, about 50 minutes. Taste and season with salt and pepper. Add the rice and continue to cook for approximately 15 minutes, until the beans and rice are tender.

Serve the peas with cornbread and cayenne hot sauce.

# Southern Green Beans

*with*
## New Potatoes

The snap and smell of fresh green beans reminds me of my grandmother's gossip. When I was a kid, those activities—listening and snapping green beans—went hand in hand. And while some might dislike the "cooked to death" Southern green beans in bacon drippings, I relish this dish on occasion.

**Makes about 4 servings**

1½   pounds (680 kg) green beans

4   slices bacon

2   pounds (910 g) small Yukon gold potatoes

Kosher salt to taste (I used about 2 teaspoons)

½   yellow onion, finely diced, as garnish (optional)

Break the beans into pieces about 1½ inches (4 cm) long. Wash and drain the beans.

In a large skillet, fry the bacon until it is crisp. Transfer the bacon to a paper-towel-lined plate, leaving as much of the drippings in the pan as you can.

Add the green beans to the hot drippings in the skillet and sauté them over medium-high heat for 3 minutes. They will lose a bit of their bright color at this point and become coated with bacon fat.

Add 4 cups water and the potatoes and bring the water to a boil over high heat. Reduce the heat to medium to simmer. Taste the beans and add salt if needed; continue simmering them in the covered but vented saucepan for about 1 hour. Taste again and adjust the seasoning. Serve them garnished with the crumbled bacon and the chopped onion if desired.

# White Beans

Always a staple on the meat-and-three line, these beans taste best spooned over cornbread with a dollop of chowchow (page 193). Melissa Corbin of Corbin in the Dell shared her family's favorite version of the dish.

**Makes 8 to 10 servings**

2   pounds (910 g) dried Great Northern beans

1   teaspoon kosher salt

2   tablespoons extra-virgin olive oil

1   teaspoon dried thyme

½   teaspoon black pepper

1   smoked ham hock

1   onion, chopped

4   cloves garlic, minced

4   cups (960 ml) chicken stock

2   bay leaves

Rinse the beans and place them in a large stockpot. Cover them with approximately 8 cups of water and stir in ½ teaspoon of the salt. Bring the water to a boil and immediately remove the pot from the heat. Cover the pot and let the beans soak overnight.

The next day, drain and rinse the beans.

In a Dutch oven or large stockpot, heat the olive oil, thyme, and pepper on medium-high. Stir in the ham hock and onion. As the onions become translucent, add the garlic and stir just long enough for the garlic to become aromatic. Add the chicken stock and 4 cups (960 ml) water. Bring to a boil before adding the beans and the bay leaves.

Once the soup is at a rolling boil, continue boiling the soup for 30 minutes and then cover and simmer it on low for 2 hours, stirring occasionally. Uncover and simmer it for 1 hour longer. Taste and stir in the remaining ½ teaspoon salt if needed. Remove the bay leaves before serving.

# Mashed Potatoes

Entire books have been written on the ways to make mashed potatoes. But my favorite version, from Nashville personal chef Jaime Miller, has a tiny tang of Greek yogurt.

**Makes about 6 to 8 servings**

4   to 5 pounds (1.8 to 2.3 kg) Yukon gold potatoes, peeled and diced

8   cups (1.9 L) chicken stock

½   cup (1 stick/115 g) butter

2   tablespoons Greek yogurt

Sea salt and black pepper

Place the potatoes in a large stockpot and pour in the chicken stock. Add water if needed to cover the potatoes. Bring the liquid to a boil. Turn the heat down to a simmer and allow the potatoes to cook until they are soft, about 15 minutes.

Drain the potatoes, leaving a little bit of the liquid—a tablespoon or two—in the pot. Return the potatoes to the pot and add the butter. Mash until the mixture is combined. If you have a stand mixer, you can mix them for a little while with the paddle attachment, but be careful not to overwork them (they'll turn gluey). Then stir in the Greek yogurt. Add salt and pepper to taste before serving.

# Bourbon Sweet Potatoes

Sweet potatoes and bourbon make good partners, and the inspiration for this pairing comes from a 1979 collection of recipes called *Nashville: 200 Years of Hospitality,* a collection by the Tennessee Federation of Women's Clubs, Inc. This sassed-up sweet potato dish fits in fine on the holiday table, showcasing the simplicity of sweet potatoes dressed up with butter, cream, bourbon, orange zest, and nutmeg—no sugary marshmallow necessary.

**Makes 8 to 10 servings**

4   pounds (1.8 kg) sweet potatoes

4   tablespoons (55 g) butter, melted

¼   cup (60 ml) heavy cream

½   cup (120 ml) bourbon

⅓   cup (80 ml) orange juice

1   teaspoon orange zest

¼   cup firmly packed (55 g) dark brown sugar

1   teaspoon sea salt

¼   teaspoon ground nutmeg

¾   cup (75 g) pecan halves

Preheat the oven to 350°F (175°C).

Peel, wash, and quarter the sweet potatoes. Place them in a stockpot, add enough water to cover them by 2 inches (5 cm), and bring them to a boil. Continue boiling them until they are fork-tender, about 15 minutes. Drain and transfer them to a large bowl.

Add the butter, cream, bourbon, orange juice, orange zest, brown sugar, salt, and nutmeg, and mash everything together with a potato masher or an electric mixer. Spoon the sweet potato mixture into a casserole dish and top it with pecan halves. Bake it for 30 minutes.

# THE RECIPES

——

# Put-Ups

# Put-Ups

# Put-Ups

# T

o the old souls, DIY types, and those who enjoy the taste of a summer blackberry in February, the *ping, ping, ping* of the lids sealing on canning jars sounds like the tiny ringing of happy bells.

Preserving food does take a little time, but it feels good, like taking care of ourselves and the ones we love. It's a practice in resourcefulness, preparedness, and restraint—saving a bit for later, making the most of what you have while it's fresh, and not wasting it. And it comes with the reward of pulling down a jar of pickles or jam preserved at the peak of the season.

The art of preserving has turned into full-fledged businesses for some in Middle Tennessee. Gary and Cortney Baron started Nashville Jam Company in 2010 to sell jams and jellies made from their home-grown produce at the local farmers' markets. When their operation grew too large to run out of their home, they moved to the Cumberland Culinary Center in Lebanon, Tennessee, where they went from filling hundreds of jars a day to thousands.

DIY food activist Sandor Katz, also based just a little more than an hour outside Nashville, preserves fruits and vegetables by fermentation. He reminds us to go beyond jam and jellies for sauerkraut and pickles, both of which you'll find recipes for in this section, along with basic strawberry jam and peppery peach preserves. Old-time recipes for chowchow, and watermelon rind pickles round out the list plus two ways to preserve ramps, also known as wild leeks or spring onions.

On a winter night, there's nothing better than the time travel that happens when you pull down a jar of preserved summer okra and peppers to make the cool nights warm again.

## KITCHEN PLAYLIST

This playlist celebrates a different kind of craft—guitar playing. In Nashville, you need not look far to find some of the best players in the world, and sometimes they are literally in a backyard.

**My Old Friend**
JACK PEARSON

With his knowledge of blues, jazz, and rock and smooth style, Pearson is a nationally recognized Nashville-based player.

**Patricia**
GUTHRIE TRAPP

This session and solo artist has worked with people like Dolly Parton, Lyle Lovett, Vince Gill, John Oates, and many more.

**Sweet Dreams**
JIM OBLON

He has worked as Paul Simon's drummer, but it's Oblon's guitar playing that has many musicians flocking to his shows in town.

**Country Music Got a Hold on Me**
KENNY VAUGHAN

Raised on his father's jazz record collection, Kenny Vaughan has had stints playing country to punk rock before moving to Nashville in 1987. He was part of the revitalization of the downtown honky-tonk scene in the 1990s before hitting the road to play with Lucinda Williams for several years and starting a band with Marty Stuart.

# Bells Bend Farms

———

———

Eric Wooldridge kicks up a growing movement among young farmers.

# Fruit grows best when connected to strong roots, and the same can be said for communities.

At the Tuesday potlucks on Bells Bend Farms, members of their community-supported agriculture (CSA) program come together with growers and neighbors to celebrate their harvests and kitchen creations of the week.

On one summer evening, magenta-colored beets and casseroles ruffled with curly greens line a long table under an open-air farm shed. Women with hair tied in scarves and men in camo caps mingle among the toddlers and hound dogs.

Milwant Sandhu, one of the elders of the community, with his white beard and indigo turban, talks about the healing properties of little-known weeds. And before I can meet his wife, Upinder, she has already handed me a Pyrex dish of black chickpeas fragrant with curry. "Carry this to the table," she says sweetly.

The fact that anyone gathers on this farm is a testament to the determination it takes to keep farmland protected. Tucked into the fertile U-shaped curve of the Cumberland River, Bells Bend has a long agricultural history. But in 2009, developers nearly succeeded in rezoning the land for five thousand homes, among other projects.

Doctors Brenda Butka and Tom John, who lived in a nearby farmhouse but knew nothing about actual farming at the time, decided they had to do something to save the land. As word got out, neighbors showed up in sleet and snow to help them start a farm. Expensive equipment and posts for fencing appeared as donations. Jeff Poppen, a sage expert known as the Barefoot Farmer of Long Hungry Creek Farm, offered to mentor them.

That's also when Eric Wooldridge stepped up. Eric had grown up down the road from Brenda and Tom. So at just twenty-two, he volunteered to work as farm manager with virtually no experience.

These days the farm has a thriving CSA program, stands at several farmers' markets across the city, and produce on plates at the city's best restaurants, such as Husk and Flyte World Dining and Wine.

At the weekly potluck, visitors scrawl the names of dishes onto scraps of notebook paper and place them beside their offerings—bowls of Brussels sprouts next to plates of goat cheese drizzled with honey and flecked with orange zest. Before lining up to eat, Brenda gathers the group in a circle and reads the Ted Hughes poem "Fern." She asks Milwant to bless the meal. He bows into a Hindu chant. "Translation?" he says after lifting his eyes. "Let it be."

As guests and workers eat, Eric, a soft-spoken man with ruddy cheeks and the weary demeanor of someone who had planted sweet corn and watermelon all day, takes a minute to relax.

"The idea was to revive this agricultural community here," he says. And sure enough, many of the young farmers who finish the night by bringing out mandolins and fiddles to play old-time tunes under the stars also have their own operations nearby—the Old School Farm, Six Boots Growers' Collective, and Goat Tender.

Here in the crook of the Cumberland, they're proving that these roots are not only strong—they're spreading.

# Strawberry Jam

These days you can find strawberry jams with basil or balsamic. But I like this simplest of versions for quickly making a batch with what's left of the early summer berry crop in Tennessee. This jam tastes perfect with Phila's Make-Do Biscuits (page 18).

**Makes enough to fill about three 4-ounce (130-ml) jars**

1 pound (455 g) strawberries, stems removed, chopped into small pieces and then crushed with potato masher

2 tablespoons fresh lemon juice

1 cup (200 g) sugar

Combine the strawberries, lemon juice, and sugar in a saucepan and cook the mixture over low heat until the sugar is dissolved. Then bring it to a boil. Continue to gently boil the jam, skimming off any foam that rises to the top and stirring until thickened, 10 to 12 minutes.

Prepare the jars as described below. While the jars are still warm, fill them with jam, leaving about ½ inch (12 mm) of room at the top. Place the lids on the jars and allow the jam to cool before refrigerating it.

## Prepping the Jars

Prepare the jars by placing them in a large stockpot. Cover the jars with water and bring it to a gentle boil. Allow the jars to sterilize in the boiling water for 15 minutes. Remove them with clean tongs and place them on a surface covered with clean towels. Remove the water from the heat and drop in the lids and rings. The jars should be hot when you fill them.

# Peppered Peach Preserves

The peppers give these preserves kick, so I love them with toast for breakfast as well as spooned over ice cream for dessert.

**Makes enough to fill about seven 8-ounce (250-ml) jars**

14 peaches

5 cups (1 kg) sugar

1 jalapeño pepper, seeds removed, chopped

½ teaspoon crushed red pepper

1 tablespoon butter

To peel the peaches, score each one with a shallow X on the bottom side. Prepare an ice bath by filling a large bowl with water and ice. Bring a large pot of water to a boil. Lower the peaches into the boiling water for just 45 seconds, then place them in the ice bath. You will be able to grasp the skins at the X and peel them off easily. Pit and chop the peaches.

Prepare the jars following instructions on page 182.

Meanwhile, combine the peaches, sugar, jalapeño, red pepper, and butter in a large saucepan. Bring the peach mixture to a boil and then reduce the heat to medium-low and simmer for 10 minutes.

While the jars are still warm, fill them with the preserves, leaving about ½ inch (12 mm) of room at the top. Place the lids on the jars and secure rings until they are "finger-tight."

Return the jars to the stockpot and add enough water to cover them by about 2 inches (5 cm). Bring it to a gentle boil for about 10 minutes. Remove the jars from the water and place them on a towel on the counter. Allow to cool to room temperature.

# Pepper Jelly

Red peppers and green jalapeños give this spicy jelly a mix of colors and textures. Spoon it over cream cheese and serve it with crackers for a classic Southern appetizer.

**Makes enough to fill about six 8-ounce (250-ml) jars**

| | |
|---|---|
| 4 | red bell peppers, seeds removed, finely chopped |
| 5 | large jalapeño peppers, seeds removed, finely chopped |
| 1 | teaspoon crushed red pepper |
| 1 | cup (240 ml) white vinegar |
| 1 | package (1.75 ounces/49 g) fruit pectin |
| ½ | teaspoon butter |
| 4 | cups (800 g) granulated sugar |

Prepare the jars following instructions on page 182.

While the jars are sterilizing, add the peppers, crushed red pepper flakes, and vinegar to a large saucepan over medium heat. Stir in the pectin and bring the mixture to a boil. Add the butter and sugar and bring it to a boil again; continue boiling for 1 minute. Remove the pan from the heat and skim any foam from the surface of the jelly.

Fill the sterilized jars with pepper jelly, leaving about ½ inch (12 mm) of room at the top. Attach the lids and rings. Return the jars to the stockpot and add enough water to cover them by about 2 inches (5 cm). Bring it to a gentle boil for about 10 minutes. Remove the jars from the water and place them on a towel on the counter. Allow to cool to room temperature.

Stephen Rose grew up in
Fort Valley, Georgia, home
to Pearson Farms, the oldest
peach-growing operation in
the state. As a friend to the
Pearson family, he asked if
he could truck peaches into
Nashville in small loads and
sell them on the streets.

During the growing season, Rose keeps Nashville in peaches, and inspires recipes in homes and restaurants across the city with The Peach Truck.

# Blackberry, Honey, Black Pepper, and Thyme Jam

Choosing honey rather than cane sugar for this magenta jam makes it a better fit for the herbs and touch of black pepper. A bit more tart than typical jam, it's also more multipurpose. Try it drizzled over cream cheese or goat cheese, and even spooned over roasted chicken or grilled salmon.

**Makes enough to fill about two 8-ounce (250-ml) jars**

| | |
|---|---|
| 1½ | pounds (680 kg) blackberries |
| | Juice of ½ lemon |
| ¼ | cup (60 ml) honey |
| 1 | teaspoon thyme leaves |
| ¼ | teaspoon black pepper |

Prepare the jars following instructions on page 182.

Meanwhile, combine the blackberries, lemon, honey, thyme, and pepper. Bring the jam to a boil and then reduce the heat to medium-low and simmer for 20 minutes or until it is thickened.

While the jars are still warm, fill them with jam, leaving about ½ inch (12 mm) of room at the top. Place the lids on the jars and secure rings. Return the jars to the stockpot and add enough water to cover them by about 2 inches (5 cm). Bring it to a gentle boil for about 10 minutes. Remove the jars from the water and place them on a towel on the counter. Allow to cool to room temperature.

# Quick Pickled Okra

Okra comes around for just a moment in summer, so I like to know I can quick-pickle it to enjoy it on the appetizer tray right away. Serve them as nibbles with cheese straws (page 46) or nuts.

**Makes about 16 appetizer servings**

- 3 cups (720 ml) cider vinegar
- 3 tablespoons granulated sugar
- 2 bay leaves
- ½ tablespoon mustard seed
- ½ tablespoon coriander seed
- 1 teaspoon crushed red pepper
- 6 tablespoons (90 g) kosher salt
- 1 pound (455 g) okra

In a saucepan over medium heat, combine the vinegar, sugar, bay leaves, mustard, coriander, red pepper, and 3 tablespoons of the salt, stirring until dissolved. Remove the pan from the heat and cool it to room temperature.

While the brine cools, rinse the okra in a colander and trim any tough ends. Toss the okra with the remaining 3 tablespoons salt in a colander. Allow the okra to drain over the sink for 30 minutes to 1 hour.

Rinse the okra and place it in a nonreactive bowl. Pour the brine over the okra. Refrigerate it preferably overnight or at least for several hours. The okra will keep in an airtight container for a couple of weeks.

# Chow-chow

Chowchow is like the confetti of relishes: Golden-tinted slivers of cabbage spiked with red pepper get spiced and sugared for pumping up the party.

Southerners have long been slipping spoonfuls of chowchow onto the sides of their plates for dipping into between bites of roasted meats, livening up white beans with cornbread, or scattering over eggs for a vinegary boost.

But at its heart, chowchow is a make-do relish pulled together by raking through what's left of the garden; it's traditionally made just with vegetables on hand. The recipe here includes a few classic ingredients such as cabbage, peppers, green tomato, onion, and spices including turmeric and mustard seed.

But like most things born of making do, chowchow's uncertain roots leave lots of leeway for creativity and just enough tradition to keep it real.

**Makes enough to fill eight 1 pint (250-ml) jars**

½ large head cabbage, finely shredded

4 green bell peppers, chopped into very small dice

4 red bell peppers, chopped into very small dice

4 yellow onions, finely chopped

6 green tomatoes, chopped

⅓ cup (80 g) kosher salt

2 cups (290 g) lightly packed light brown sugar

2 cups (480 ml) cider vinegar

2 teaspoons celery seeds

1 teaspoon dry mustard

1 tablespoon mustard seeds

1 teaspoon ground turmeric

½ teaspoon ground ginger

½ teaspoon crushed red pepper

In a large bowl, combine the cabbage with the other chopped vegetables—bell peppers, onions, and tomatoes.

In a large pot, mix the salt, sugar, and vinegar and bring the mixture to a boil, stirring until the sugar dissolves. Add the celery seeds, dry mustard, mustard seeds, turmeric, ginger, and crushed red pepper and stir to combine. Then add the vegetables. Reduce the heat to medium-low and simmer for 1 hour.

Prepare the jars following instructions on page 182.

With a large spoon, pack the vegetable mixture, along with its cooking liquid, into the warm, sterile jars. With a clean, dry dishtowel, wipe the mouth of each jar. Place a lid on each jar and tighten the ring. Place the jars in boiling water for 10 minutes. Remove the jars from the water and set them aside; listen for the lids to ping, indicating that the jars have sealed. Serve the chowchow chilled or at room temperature.

# Water- melon Rind Pickles

Some of the best recipes, like this one from my friend Jesse Goldstein, come from making the most of scraps. Pickling watermelon rind turns the part you'd normally discard into a tart-sweet bite to pair with cheese and bread before the main event.

**Makes about 20 servings**

Rind from 1 watermelon

¼ cup (70 g) pickling salt

1 cup (240 ml) white vinegar

¾ cup (180 ml) cider vinegar

2 cups (400 g) granulated sugar

2 cinnamon sticks

2 star anise pods

8 whole cloves

6 allspice berries

Prepare the rind by first removing the majority of ripe fruit, leaving a small amount on the rind. Peel off the outer green skin and cut the rind into 1-inch (2.5-cm) pieces. Measure out 5 cups for pickling and place them in a heat-safe bowl (discard any extra or make a second batch of pickles).

Bring 6 cups (1.4 L) of water and the pickling salt to a boil and pour it over the watermelon rind. Let the rind sit and cool to room temperature before covering and refrigerating it overnight.

Drain the salted water from the rind. Add both vinegars and the sugar, cinnamon sticks, star anise, cloves, and allspice to a small saucepan over medium-high heat.

Cover and bring the mixture to a boil. Reduce the heat to a simmer and cook, covered, for 5 minutes. Pour the hot pickling syrup over the watermelon rind. Refrigerate it overnight.

Drain the pickling syrup from the rinds into a saucepan. Bring it to a boil and pour it over the rinds again; cover and refrigerate over-night. Repeat this process three to four times, until the pieces of watermelon rind no longer float in the pickling liquid.

Pickled watermelon rinds will keep for 2 to 3 weeks in an airtight container in the refrigerator.

# Sauerkraut

Charlie Nelson of Nelson's Green Brier Distillery makes sauer-kraut, translated as "sour cabbage," for his family's Thanksgiving dinners. Given the German influence in Nashville and the tradition of putting up foods to preserve them through the winter, it makes sense for a family to enjoy it over that holiday. Sauerkraut and other preserved vegetables maintained a nutritious snap when fresh vegetables proved harder to come by. The salt in this recipe helps pull the water from the cabbage, creating a brine for fermentation.

Mixing green and red cabbage makes for a dramatic, hot-pink version with red chile and caraway seeds for kick.

**Makes about 12 servings**

½   **head red cabbage**

½   **head green cabbage**

1   **red onion, sliced**

1½   **tablespoons sea salt**

1   **teaspoon caraway seeds**

½   **teaspoon crushed red pepper**

Make sure the equipment you use and your hands are very clean. Combine all the ingredients in a large bowl and, using your hands, massage the salt into the cabbage and onion for about 5 minutes to begin the release of water.

Place the cabbage mixture in a large nonreactive bowl or crock with a wide mouth. Cover the cabbage with a plate that just fits inside the container and set a weight—such as a jug of water—on top to keep the cabbage submerged. Cover the container with a cloth.

Store the cabbage in a cool place, checking it periodically. The liquid should rise above the plate within 24 hours. After 2 more days, the sauerkraut will have developed a tangy taste. Allow the cabbage to sit in the liquid for 4 weeks, checking it daily to make sure it's submerged and skimming off any scum. Transfer it to a sterile glass container with a lid and store it in the refrigerator for up to 6 months.

# Preserved Ramp Greens

When Chef Matt Bolus, a Tennessee native, worked at FIG restaurant in Charleston, he took a liking to working with ramps, wild leeks with a strong onion/leek/garlic flavor. So on trips back to his home state, he started regular ramp-hunting adventures with ham maker Allan Benton of Smoky Mountain Country Hams, a fellow ramp aficionado. Now, any season, he has an abundance of ramps at his restaurant in Nashville, preserved in various ways. "I like to use them simply sautéed," he says of the ramps preserved in oil. "You cut them into a few sections right out of the jar and put them in the pan. Delightful with scrambled eggs."

He adds that you can use the oil to sauté other ingredients, like potatoes, or whisk it into salad dressing.

**Makes enough to fill about eight 8-ounce (250-ml) jars**

2 pounds (910 g) ramp greens, washed and patted dry

**Extra-virgin olive oil**

Divide the ramp greens into eight equal piles.

Stack the greens up lengthwise and tightly roll up each pile so that they will fit into the jars, leaving about ½ inch (12 mm) of space at the top.

Carefully add olive oil until it just covers the greens. You will have to do this several times as air escapes and the oil soaks into the spaces between the greens. You can speed up the process by lightly tapping the bottoms of the jars to help dislodge the bubbles.

Once the jars are filled with oil, completely covering the ramp greens, close the jars with the lids and rings, and refrigerate them overnight.

The next day, open each of the jars to make sure the greens are still covered in oil. Add more oil if needed and reseal the jars. Place them in the freezer and keep them for up to a year.

When you want to use the greens, it is best to allow them to thaw overnight in the refrigerator. Both the greens and oil can be served.

# Pickled Ramps

Serve Chef Matt Bolus's pickled version of this wild onion alongside grilled meats or add them to your cheese plates. They also add punch to warming bowls of beans.

**Makes enough to fill two quart (1-L) jars**

1 tablespoon kosher salt

1 cup (240 ml) white wine vinegar

1 cup (240 ml) sorghum syrup

2 teaspoons yellow mustard seeds

2 teaspoons Szechuan peppercorns

2 teaspoons coriander seeds

1 teaspoon fennel seeds

½ teaspoon crushed red pepper (optional)

6 sprigs fresh thyme

2 bay leaves

2 pounds (910 g) ramp bulbs, all greens removed

Prepare the jars following instructions on page 182.

Combine the salt, vinegar, sorghum, mustard seeds, peppercorns, coriander seeds, fennel seeds, red pepper flakes, and thyme in a stainless-steel pot and bring the mixture to a boil. Whisk until the sorghum and salt have completely dissolved.

Place a bay leaf in each jar and then divide the ramp bulbs between the jars, packing them so that there is roughly 1 inch (2.5 cm) of room at the top.

While the pickling liquid is still hot, carefully fill each jar, just covering the ramps completely.

Put the lids and rings on the jars. Be careful not to tighten the rings down.

Process the jars in boiling water for 10 minutes. Carefully remove the jars from the boiling water, place them on a towel on the counter, and allow to cool to room temperature.

# House Dill Pickles

Brian Jackson of the Atomic Yardbirds hunts, forages, bakes, and cans. His pickles pair well with his award-winning Nashville-style hot chicken (page 68).

**Makes enough to fill two wide-mouth quart (1-L) jars**

⅔ cup (165 ml) white vinegar

¼ cup plus ½ teaspoon (75 g) pickling salt

A fistful of fresh dill, both fronds and stems

6 cloves garlic

10 firm Kirby cucumbers

Prepare the jars following instructions on page 182.

In a medium saucepan, bring 2½ cups (600 ml) water, the vinegar, and ¼ cup (72 g) of the pickling salt to a boil. Turn off the heat and set the pan aside.

Place a layer of dill at the bottom of each jar, along with two garlic cloves, then tightly pack the cucumbers into the jar, filling it up to the neck (depending on the size of the cucumbers, you may get two nice layers with a few small cucumbers at the top). Add more dill and another garlic clove at the top. Add ¼ teaspoon pickling salt to each jar (this makes for a crunchier pickle). Once the jars are loaded, pour in the brine, leaving ½ inch (12 mm) of room at the top.

Wipe the top of the jar and the threads clean with a wet cloth. Tighten the lid and ring onto each jar. Place the jars into a canner, with the water level just to the necks of the jars. Bring the water almost to a boil (this will take about 15 minutes). Remove the jars using clean tongs, set them on a dishtowel spread on the counter, and let them cool. Tighten the rings once cool.

Allow the pickles to rest for a few weeks to completely cure before serving them.

## THE RECIPES

———

# SWEETS

# *Sweets*

# SWEETS

# B

art Pickens, former chef at the Loveless Cafe, likes to make the first bite of bread and last bite of dessert the most fabulous. Because if you kiss them first and last, he says, they'll remember you.

It's appropriate that a chef at a Nashville institution known for its biscuits and cobblers and pies would make such a claim. They have this romance locked up.

For that last kiss, the Loveless often entrusted long-time pastry chef Alisa Huntsman. She would make ramekins of cobbler with jewel-colored fruit lava bubbling under a biscuity surface, or cool, creamy peanut butter pies with a cloud of whipped cream on top and a foundation of crumbled homemade chocolate cookies as dark as good soil.

As she worked, baking her own vanilla wafers to crumble for crusts and drizzling the tops of pies in perfect zigzags, she could tell you that the Southern sweet tooth is hardly a myth. Prod a group of Southerners to wax poetic over food, and they'll likely remember the toasty meringue on an aunt's banana pudding or a favorite roadside hand pie oozing with apple filling.

The recipes in this section tap into those old favorites, including a classic and easy blackberry cobbler and banana pudding, as well as more modern versions of desserts that bridge the gap between past and present.

And a couple recipes make the best of two Nashville favorites: Goo Goo Clusters, the candy bar founded in 1912, and Olive and Sinclair, the bean-to-bar chocolate company created a century later.

## KITCHEN PLAYLIST

Sweets—maybe more as metaphor than as actual dessert—have long inspired songwriters, as in the Beatles' "Wild Honey Pie." The following songs about sugar have Nashville ties.

**The Black Bat Licorice**
JACK WHITE

This Nashville resident sings about the dark side of sweet, and we wouldn't expect anything less from him.

**Candy**
MARION JAMES

Nashville's queen of blues sings about her sweet tooth for her sweetheart.

**Money Maker**
THE BLACK KEYS

Honey sweetens this song by these Nashville-based rockers.

**Country Pie**
BOB DYLAN

Though he's not a Nashville artist, Dylan recorded this song in Nashville for his 1969 album *Nashville Skyline*.

# Olive and Sinclair

MAKERS OF
STONE-GROUND
CHOCOLATE
AND
FINE CANDY
PRODUCTS

An East Nashville chocolate factory turns out Southern-style sweets.

Like the chocolate elf of Nashville, Scott Witherow, founder of Olive and Sinclair, has a way that seems both deeply Southern and not of this world.

He greets guests at his East Nashville chocolate factory with a humble little bow and dimpled smile. A big personality wrapped in a small apron and funky spectacles, he speaks with an old-fashioned lilt as he leads guests into his space. And to newcomers, it's a wonderland, with machines churning chocolate and air thick with the earthy-sweet aroma of roasted and ground cacao beans. Antique signs hang on brick walls, and a cherry red neon sign urges us to eat.

"I'm a borderline hoarder," Scott says of all the signage.

But hoarding those antique treasures has benefited him when it comes to creative inspiration. An old box of shotgun shells led to the devel-opment of his popular and award-winning Duck Fat Caramels, nuggets of soft caramelized cane sugar flavored with duck fat. Other creations have been equally serendipitous, bringing together a creative mind, a careful craft, and attention to history and place that results in . . . chocolate.

Scott began experimenting with bean-to-bar chocolate making in 2006 while working as a pastry chef at F. Scott's in Nashville. He has been in the food business in some capacity since age fourteen and attended Le Cordon Bleu in London, where he also worked and staged at restaurants like the Fat Duck. But when he told his boss at F. Scott's he was striking out to make chocolate bars? "I remember him looking at me squirrely eyed, like, 'Are you sure?'" he says.

The first batch Scott made with the intention of selling, he ended up giving away at the East Nashville Tomato Art Fest. "It was not what I wanted at all. That's when we decided to put kosher salt and black pepper on it." The idea, he explained, was like doctoring up a "not-so-good tomato."

The people loved his salt-and-pepper chocolate bars, though, so he kept the idea while continuing to hone the chocolate recipe.

That was September 2009, and it didn't take long for Olive and Sinclair to take the lead as one of the city's first small-batch artisans in the modern resurgence of makers across the country.

Beyond the salt-and-pepper bars, he developed sea salt chocolate and Mexican-style cinnamon chili. And he's also created several products that capture the creative spirit of Nashville by showcasing other makers in the open collaboration that happens across the city. For example, he ages cacao beans in Corsair Distillery bourbon barrels for his Bourbon Nib Brittle bar. He also smokes nibs at Allan Benton's ham smokehouse for the Smoked Nib Brittle bar. "We like the friendships and alliances we've been able to form," he says. When those products came to be, there wasn't a particular plan or end goal in mind, it was just an experiment to see where it would lead.

Allan Benton had told him, "Scott, you ought to send me some of those cacao beans and let me put them in my smokehouse and see what happens." And similarly, Andrew Webber of Corsair told him, "I've got a bunch of Triple Smoke (whiskey) barrels in my truck. You want them?" All of it happened naturally, and Scott, though admittedly biased as a native Middle Tennessean, says it comes genuinely in this town.

But if you ask Scott and his team (of still just a handful of employees), they'll say that perhaps the most underappreciated aspect of their chocolate goes back to the brown sugar. "It's not just a bells-and-whistles thing," Scott said. "It allows our chocolate to have a slower sweet warm-up. It also gives it the molassesy undertones that kind of marry much better with the fruit notes in chocolate."

He says it's the same with the buttermilk in his Buttermilk White bar. It was more than just a Southern thing; buttermilk acts as an acid to balance the sweetness and fattiness of the other ingredients in white chocolate. He also uses the salt and pepper in the white chocolate in place of vanilla. "I think vanilla takes over in white chocolate, and salt and pepper act as more of a backbone," he says.

With his latest confection line called Seersucker, Scott offers a truffled bourbon ball and a pickled cherry bomb, and he keeps packing creativity and Southern story into every bite.

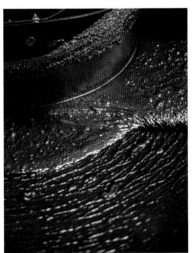

After roasting and separating cocoa
nibs from their shells, the nibs go into
machines that were built in the early
1900s, which press them under the
weight of rollers.

The chocolate tempers after brown sugar has been added. Then the mixture is molded into bars, cooled, and hand-wrapped.

# Olive and Sinclair Double Chocolate Pound Cake

This recipe aims to showcase Olive and Sinclair chocolate in a cake filled with big hunks of the rich, dark bars.

**Makes 1 loaf**

1¼ cups (155 g) all-purpose flour

½ cup (40 g) cocoa powder

½ teaspoon baking powder

¼ teaspoon baking soda

½ teaspoon sea salt

1 cup (2 sticks/225 g) butter plus more for pan

1 cup (145 g) light brown sugar

½ cup plus 2 tablespoons (125 g) granulated sugar

2 large eggs

⅓ cup (80 ml) whole milk

⅔ cup (165 ml) sour cream

2 teaspoons vanilla extract

5 ounces (150 g) Olive and Sinclair 67 percent cacao chocolate, roughly chopped

Preheat the oven to 350°F (175°C). Lightly butter a loaf pan and line it with parchment paper.

In a medium bowl, combine the flour, cocoa powder, baking powder, baking soda, and salt.

In a second medium bowl, cream together the butter, brown sugar, and ½ cup (100 g) of the granulated sugar. Add the eggs one at a time, stirring well after each. Add the milk, sour cream, and vanilla.

Pour the dry ingredients into the wet ingredients and combine. Fold in about two-thirds of the chocolate pieces.

Pour the batter into the prepared pan and top it with the remaining chocolate and 2 tablespoons of granulated sugar. Bake the cake for 1 hour or until a toothpick inserted in the center comes out clean. Serve it for dessert—or breakfast.

# Chess Pie

Some recipes for this Southern classic call for milk or cream, which makes less of a translucent pie. This version sticks with just eggs, sugar, and butter, as well as the key ingredients for tang and texture: vinegar and cornmeal.

And while this version is clearer in appearance, the story behind the dessert's name is not. Chess pie could be short for "chest," as pies were once kept in a pie chest or pie safe cupboard. Another story suggests this simple pie created from what's on hand might have at one time been called "just pie," which over the years became "jus' pie" and then "chess pie."

**Makes 1 pie**

1¼ cups (250 g) sugar

1 tablespoon cornmeal

½ cup (1 stick/115 g) butter, melted and cooled

3 large eggs, lightly beaten

1 teaspoon vanilla extract

1 teaspoon white vinegar

1 (9-inch/23-cm) piecrust

Whipped cream and berries for serving (optional)

Preheat the oven to 350°F (175°C). In a medium mixing bowl, combine the sugar and cornmeal. Add the butter, eggs, vanilla, and vinegar. Stir to combine, then pour the filling into the piecrust.

Bake the pie for about 45 minutes, until the filling is set and it turns golden brown on top.

Serve the pie with a dollop of whipped cream and berries if desired.

# Cherry Hand Pies

Lisa Donovan, who has worked as a pastry chef at Husk Nashville, Margot Café and Bar, and City House, celebrates Southern ingredients and desserts like bourbon butterscotch pudding, buttermilk pies, and layered Lane cake. "Tradition is everything for me," she says. "I'm drawn to recipes that have an emotional hold on me." She scours old recipe books, church cookbooks, and "Meemaw recipes," as she calls them.

She prefers a hand pie to a fried pie, and her recipe for the pie crust below can work in larger pies as well. Lisa also takes some of the pressure off in making this recipe by suggesting that bakers use prepared, good-quality fruit preserves on occasion, such as this version with cherry preserves.

**Makes 9 hand pies**

| | |
|---|---|
| 3 | cups plus 3 tablespoons (395 g) all-purpose flour |
| 2 ½ | teaspoons kosher salt |
| 10 ½ | ounces (2 ¼ sticks/280 g) butter, cut into ½-inch (12-mm) cubes and chilled |
| | Ice water |
| | Cherry preserves |
| 1 | large egg, beaten |
| | Coarse white sugar for sprinkling |

Preheat the oven to 350°F (175°C).

In a large mixing bowl, combine the flour and salt. Remove the butter from the refrigerator or freezer and, using your fingers, quickly work it into the flour until the consistency of the mixture is partly mealy, with a few almond-size hunks of butter.

Add ice water, beginning with ¼ cup (60 ml), then adding it by tablespoons, just until the dough forms a moist but somewhat shaggy ball. Turn the dough out onto a floured surface to knead very gently until it comes together. Wrap it in plastic and chill it for at least 30 minutes.

Place the chilled dough on a lightly floured surface and cut it into two pieces. Working with one piece at a time, roll out the dough and cut it into circles about 4 inches (10 cm) in diameter.

Place a tablespoon of preserves just right of center on each circle. Brush egg along edge of one side of each circle. Fold the dough over the preserves. Press the edges together with the tines of a fork to seal them. Brush the tops of the pies with more egg and sprinkle them with the sugar.

Place the pies on a baking sheet and bake them for 30 minutes, until the crust is light golden. Allow the pies to cool until just warm before serving.

# Hello Dolly Cookie Bars

2½ cups (255 g) finely crushed crumbs from your favorite cookies, such as graham crackers

½ teaspoon salt

½ cup (1 stick/115 g) unsalted butter, melted

6 ounces (170 g) chopped semisweet chocolate or chocolate chips

3 ounces (85 g) unsweetened shredded coconut

1 cup (115 g) chopped pecans

1 (14-ounce/396-g) can sweetened condensed milk

As a pastry chef living in modern times, Rebekah Turshen of City House often takes photos and posts her latest creations on social media, giving diners a peek at how they could end their meals at the restaurant. But even with the advancements in technology at hand, her ingredients are often as old-fashioned as it gets.

"It's pawpaw season!" she wrote of the mango-looking fruit with the texture and taste of banana. "Tonight only!" The pawpaw pies arrive in individual servings, sitting in an artful puddle of lemon marmalade, with a tuft of lime cream on top, speckled with poppy-seed-cornmeal cookie crumbs. She both revives old-fashioned treats, like lemon chess pies with strawberry preserves, and makes mass-produced favorites from scratch, like Tennessee-native Moon Pies. She always works that spark of nostalgic recognition to add something unexpected. That might mean using a technique not readily available to the home cook or creating a dessert that's a bit less sweet by incorporating an extra note of salt or an interesting texture to bring out the best of what we love about an old favorite.

But when she wants a crowd-pleasing cookie bar for Red Barn Roundup potlucks (more on page 126), she chooses the Hello Dolly. Tandy Wilson, the chef at City House, gave her his grandmother's recipe for these bars. Rebekah has made it her own, but she jokes that even though it has passed through many hands, it could have originated on the back of a can of sweetened condensed milk.

"Hello Dollys are user-friendly bars," she says. "Feel free to experiment with any cookies, nuts, and chocolate you have on hand. The coconut is optional as well. You can take it out and add a bit of extra chocolate or nuts if you like."

**Makes 32 bite-size squares**

Preheat the oven to 325°F (165°C).

In a medium bowl, combine the cookie crumbs, salt, and melted butter. Scatter the mixture onto a parchment-lined 8-inch (20-cm) square baking pan. Press the cookie mixture flat into the pan.

In another medium bowl, combine the chocolate, coconut, and pecans, and scatter the mixture over the crust.

Drizzle the condensed milk across the top. Bake the bars for 25 to 30 minutes or until they turn a light caramel color.

Let the bars cool and then cut them into squares to serve.

# Sorghum Bourbon Pecan Pie

The slightly mineral tastes of sorghum syrup, made from sorghum cane, pairs well with the salt and butter of biscuits—and pie dough. Using sorghum rather than cane syrup for pecan pie also makes the sweet in this classic pie more interesting.

**Makes 1 pie**

| | |
|---|---|
| 1 | cup (200 g) sugar |
| 2 | tablespoon butter, melted |
| ½ | cup (120 ml) sorghum syrup |
| 3 | large eggs |
| 2 | tablespoons bourbon |
| 1 | teaspoon vanilla extract |
| ¼ | teaspoon sea salt |
| 1½ | cups (170 g) pecans |
| 1 | (9-inch/23-cm) piecrust |
| | Fresh whipped cream for garnish (optional) |

Preheat the oven to 350°F (175°C).

In a medium bowl, combine the sugar, butter, sorghum, eggs, bourbon, vanilla, and salt. Stir in the pecans.

Pour the filling into the piecrust. Bake the pie for 1 hour or until the middle feels set when you press on it lightly. (Check the pie after about 40 minutes. If the edges of the crust are getting too brown, you might want to fold strips of aluminum foil around them to shield them from the heat.)

Allow the pie to cool for about 2 hours before slicing it. Serve it with a dollop of fresh whipped cream if desired.

# Goo Goo Cluster Frozen Pie

Before 1912, candy bars were just that—a bar of a single type of candy such as chocolate or taffy. But that year on First Avenue in Nashville, using a copper cauldron, a man named Howell Campbell created the Goo Goo Cluster, believed to be the first combination candy bar.

Merchants displayed the mounds of pillowy marshmallow and chunky nuts, draped in caramel and dunked in chocolate, behind a glass case and hand-wrapped them with each sale. Eventually they were mass-produced by the Standard Candy Co., and the bars became an integral brand in Nashville life as sponsor of the Grand Ole Opry. Their live commercials proclaimed, "Go Get a Goo Goo. It's gooooooood!" When director Robert Altman included the jingle in his film *Nashville,* Hollywood executives believed he had made it up.

Many believed "Goo" to be an acronym for Grand Ole Opry, but the origin of the candy's name remains unknown.

The candy celebrated its hundred-year-anniversary in 2012, and it inspired at least forty creations from local chefs, cooks, and bartenders, including chocolate martinis and this recipe for Goo Goo frozen pie from McCabe Pub, a favorite neighborhood restaurant and bar in Sylvan Park.

As the jingle affirms, the Goo Goo is good, and even after a hundred years, it's far from gone, too.

**Makes 1 pie**

2   cups (480 ml) heavy cream

1   cup (100 g) confectioner's sugar

1   teaspoon vanilla extract

2   tablespoons bourbon

4   Goo Goo Clusters, chopped

1   (9-inch/23-cm) graham cracker crust

Using a mixer and a large bowl, whip the cream until stiff peaks form. Reduce the speed to low and add the sugar, vanilla, and bourbon, mixing until fully blended. Fold half of the chopped Goo Goo Clusters in by hand, mixing well.

Spread the filing into the crust. Top it with the remaining Goo Goo Cluster pieces. Freeze the pie until it is firm, about 4 hours, or overnight. Serve pie in frozen slices.

# Blackberry Cobbler

There are many ways to make a cobbler, such as biscuit dough plopped like heavy cumulus clouds on top of berry and fruit combinations. But when I asked my friend Jaime Miller how she likes to make it, she spouted off the cuppa-cuppa method as if I were crazy not to already know it. Cup of sugar, cup of flour, stick of butter, and hardly much else. It's also similar to the one Truvy (Dolly Parton) describes to Clairee (Olympia Dukakis) in *Steel Magnolias.*

And so with close friends and Dolly behind the cuppa method, it's been my favorite ever since. Beyond the ease of this recipe, it's also an excellent version, making a cake that's gooey down toward the fruit and perfect with a scoop of ice cream.

**Makes about 12 servings**

- 2 cups (290 g) blackberries
- 1 tablespoon lemon juice
- Pinch ground cinnamon
- ½ cup (1 stick/115 g) butter, melted
- 1 cup (125 g) self-rising flour
- 1 cup (200 g) granulated sugar
- 1 cup (240 ml) whole milk
- Pinch salt
- Ice cream for serving

Preheat the oven to 350°F (175°C). Grease a 9-inch (23-cm) deep-dish pie plate.

In a medium bowl, combine the blackberries with the lemon juice and cinnamon.

In another medium bowl, combine the butter with the flour, sugar, milk, and salt. Stir the mixture together—it's okay if it's still a little lumpy.

Pour the batter into the prepared pie plate. Spread the berries on top of the batter.

Bake the cobbler for 30 to 40 minutes or until it is bubbling and golden on top. Serve it with ice cream.

# Boozy Baked Peaches

I learned about cooking peaches in a muffin tin from a 1977 edition of the Nashville Junior League cookbook, *Nashville Seasons Encore*. It's a smart way to keep the fruit upright and the gooey filling from spilling over the sides.

The bourbon and butter in this recipe help soften the gingersnaps to create a rich, boozy center for the peaches. They'll need nothing more when they come out of the oven, but if you're feeling fancy, add a dollop of crème fraîche and a shake of cinnamon to garnish.

**Makes 6 servings**

| | |
|---|---|
| 3 | peaches, halved and pitted |
| 6 | gingersnap cookies, broken into pieces |
| 1½ | teaspoons light brown sugar |
| 2 | tablespoons chopped pecans |
| 2 | tablespoons bourbon |
| 2 | tablespoons butter, melted |
| | Crème fraîche for serving (optional) |
| | Ground cinnamon for garnish (optional) |

Preheat the oven to 300°F (150°C).

Place the peach halves cut side up in the muffin tins.

In a small bowl, stir together the gingersnap pieces, brown sugar, pecans, bourbon, and butter. Spoon the mixture into the peaches and bake them for about 15 minutes.

Serve them with crème fraîche and cinnamon if you like.

# Peaches and Dumplings

8 fresh peaches, peeled, pitted, and cut into segments

Juice of 1 lemon

1½ cups (210 g) lightly packed light brown sugar

¼ teaspoon ground cardamom

1 cup (125 g) all-purpose flour

2 teaspoons baking powder

2 teaspoons granulated sugar

1 teaspoon sea salt

⅛ teaspoon freshly grated nutmeg

1 tablespoon butter

½ cup (120 ml) cream

Vanilla ice cream for serving

This recipe comes from Jesse Goldstein, also known around town as the Food Sheriff. The nickname comes from his childhood, when he appointed himself the role of divvying up the family meals to his brothers to keep things, ahem, fair. These days, it's also the namesake of his food branding company.

The chef and former brand manager at the iconic Loveless Cafe had the idea for this dish after talking with another Nashville icon, a bar owner who calls himself Santa. It's a name that fits Santa's long white beard and the way he presides over his Santa's Pub, a Christmas-themed trailer with live music, cheap beer, and karaoke.

Santa once told Jesse about a blackberry and dumpling dish he prepares, and so Jesse adapted it as follows for the peach season.

"Peach cobbler is definitely an all-time Southern favorite, but the idea of turning on the oven in the heat of peach season is not quite so popular," Jesse says. "This simple recipe can fill that cobbler craving with just one pot on the stovetop."

**Makes 6 to 8 servings**

Place 1½ cups (360 ml) water with the peaches, lemon juice, brown sugar, and cardamom in a heavy-bottomed saucepan over low heat. Cover and cook the mixture for 5 minutes on low to release the juices before raising the heat to medium-high and bringing it to a boil. Once it is boiling, reduce the temperature to maintain a moderate simmer and cook it for 8 minutes.

Meanwhile, sift the flour, baking powder, granulated sugar, and salt into a mixing bowl. Add the nutmeg. Using a pastry blender or knife, cut in the butter until the mixture is crumbly. Blend in the cream with a wooden spoon to make a soft dough.

Divide the dough in half for easier handling and roll each piece into a log about 1 inch (2.5 cm) in diameter. Using a knife, cut the logs into 1-inch (2.5-cm) pieces.

After the peaches have simmered for 8 minutes, add the dough pieces to the simmering peaches. Cover the pot and reduce the heat to a low simmer. Cook the mixture for 15 minutes. Avoid stirring during this time and watch carefully so the peaches don't boil over.

Serve the peaches and dumplings warm with a scoop of vanilla ice cream.

# Banana Pudding

Ask a Nashvillian for the best banana pudding in town, and if he knows his stuff, he'll tell you Arnold's Country Kitchen. The restaurant's version, scooped into small bowls at the cold end of the food line at the meat-and-three, isn't deconstructed or whipped into a shake or formed into cheesecake. It's just a perfect traditional banana pudding chock-full of bananas and wafers that have lost a bit of their crispness. This version, adapted from the recipe on a 1970s-era Nabisco Nilla Wafers box by home cook Barbara Davenport, reminds me of that Arnold's classic.

**Makes 10 to 12 servings**

1 cup (200 g) sugar

⅓ cup plus 2 tablespoons (55 g) all-purpose flour

Dash salt

6 large eggs, separated, at room temperature

3 cups (720 ml) whole milk

½ teaspoon vanilla extract

1 teaspoon whiskey

¼ teaspoon cinnamon

1 (11-ounce/311-g) box vanilla wafers

5 to 6 fully ripe bananas, sliced

¼ teaspoon cream of tartar

Preheat the oven to 425°F (220°C).

In the top of a double boiler, combine ¾ cup (150 g) of the sugar with the flour and salt.

In a separate bowl, mix together the 6 egg yolks and milk; beat slightly. Add the mixture to the double boiler and cook, uncovered, over boiling water, stirring constantly until it has thickened. If it is lumpy, beat it with a whisk. Reduce the heat to simmering and cook, stirring occasionally, for about 5 minutes. Remove the custard from the heat and stir in the vanilla, whiskey, and cinnamon.

In a 1½- to 2-quart (1.4- to 2-L) baking dish, spread a small amount of custard on the bottom and cover it with a layer of vanilla wafers. Top with a layer of sliced bananas. Pour about a third of the remaining custard over the bananas, and continue to layer wafers, bananas, and custard, ending with custard.

In a metal bowl, beat the egg whites and cream of tartar until they are stiff but not dry. Add the remaining sugar a little at a time until stiff peaks form. Spoon the meringue on top of the pudding, spreading it to cover the entire surface. Bake the pudding for 5 to 8 minutes or until the meringue turns golden brown. Let cool then transfer to the refrigerator. Serve the dessert chilled.

# Blackberry Jam Cake

## *with* Caramel Frosting

A traditional cake in this area, blackberry jam cake can be frosted with other types of frosting, but the caramel made with brown sugar is a favorite.

**Makes 1 layer cake**

### For the cake:

- 1 cup (2 sticks/225 g) butter, plus more for pans
- 2 cups (400 g) granulated sugar
- 3 eggs
- 1 cup (240 ml) buttermilk
- 1 teaspoon baking soda
- 1 cup (240 ml) blackberry jam
- 3½ cups (440 g) all-purpose flour
- 1 teaspoon ground cloves
- 1 teaspoon ground allspice
- 1 teaspoon ground cinnamon
- 1 cup (115 g) chopped pecans

### For the caramel frosting and garnish:

- ½ cup (1 stick/115 g) butter
- 1 cup packed (220 g) light brown sugar
- ⅓ cup (80 ml) whole milk
- About 2 cups (200 g) confectioners' sugar
- Whole pecan halves for garnish (optional)

*Prepare the cake:*
Preheat the oven to 325°F (165°C). Butter two 9-inch (23-cm) round cake pans and line the bottoms with parchment paper.

In a medium bowl, cream together the butter and sugar. Add the eggs and beat thoroughly. Add the buttermilk, baking soda, and jam.

In a separate bowl, sift together the flour, cloves, allspice, and cinnamon. Add the dry ingredients to the wet ingredients in batches, beating to combine. Stir in the pecans.

Divide the batter between the prepared pans. Bake the cakes for 40 minutes to an hour, or until a toothpick inserted in the center of the cake comes out clean. Allow them to cool for at least 15 minutes before turning them out of the pans onto a wire rack to cool completely.

*Prepare the frosting:*
In a medium saucepan, melt the butter over medium-low heat. Add the brown sugar and bring the mixture to a boil, stirring constantly, for 2 minutes. Stir in the milk and transfer the brown sugar mixture to a medium mixing bowl. Gradually add the confectioners' sugar, beating continuously, until you have a consistency for spreading that you like.

To assemble the cake, place one of the cake layers on a serving plate and spread the top with frosting (level the cake by slicing off the top with a knife if it rises higher in the middle). Stack the second layer on top of the first and spread the top with frosting. It's best to make thick layers of frosting only for tops of the layers, leaving the sides of this cake bare. Garnish the top of the cake with pecans on top if desired and serve.

# Kitty Wells–Inspired Orange Coconut Cake

Coconut layer cakes often mean there's something special to celebrate, whether it's Easter or a new baby.

Van Tucker, an excellent home cook, adapted this recipe from country singer Kitty Wells's version. One of Van's contributions was to add fresh lavender from her garden, which gives the cake a light herbal flavor that pairs perfectly with the orange.

**Makes 1 layer cake**

- ½ cup (1 stick/115 g) butter, at room temperature, plus more for pans
- 1 cup (200 g) sugar
- 1 teaspoon vanilla extract
- ¼ cup (60 ml) orange juice
- 1 tablespoon orange zest
- 1 tablespoon finely chopped lavender
- 2 eggs
- 2 cups (280 g) cake flour
- 1 teaspoon baking powder
- ¾ teaspoon baking soda
- ¼ teaspoon salt
- 1 cup (240 ml) buttermilk
- Orange coconut Frosting (recipe follows)

Preheat the oven to 350°F (175°C). Butter two 9-inch (23-cm) round cake pans.

In a medium bowl, cream the butter and sugar together. Add the vanilla, orange juice, orange zest, and lavender. Add in the eggs, one at a time, beating after each.

In a second medium bowl, sift together the cake flour, baking powder, baking soda, and salt. Add these dry ingredients to the creamed mixture, alternating with the buttermilk.

Divide the batter between the prepared pans and bake for 30 minutes. Allow the cakes to cool in the pans for 15 minutes before turning them out onto a wire rack to cool completely.

Place one of the cake layers on a serving plate (level cake by slicing off top with a knife if it rises higher in the middle) and spread the top with Orange Coconut Frosting. Stack the second layer on top of the first and spread with frosting as well as sides of cake.

## Orange Coconut Frosting

**Makes enough to frost a two-layer 9-inch (23-cm) cake**

- 1 (16-ounce/455-g) box confectioner's sugar
- ½ cup (1 stick/115 g) butter, softened
- 3 to 4 tablespoons (45 to 60 ml) orange juice
- 1 tablespoon orange zest
- 1 package (7 ounces/198 g) shredded coconut
- 1 teaspoon vanilla extract

Combine the sugar, butter, and 3 tablespoons of the orange juice and beat on medium speed for 1 to 2 minutes until creamy. Add the orange zest, coconut, and vanilla. Add additional orange juice if needed until the frosting reaches the desired consistency.

# Strawberry Buttermilk Paletas

Irma and Norma Paz, sisters who came to Nashville from Mexico, inspired this recipe with their popular Mexican ice pop business, Las Paletas. The sisters opened their shop in the Twelfth South district long before it had turned into the hip hangout it is today. Though Irma and Norma offer flavors like avocado, coconut, and cantaloupe, this recipe in particular celebrates a couple favorite ingredients in this area—sweet strawberries and tangy buttermilk.

**Makes about 6 ice pops**

- 1½ cups (360 ml) buttermilk
- ½ cup (120 ml) full-fat Greek yogurt
- 1 cup (240 ml) mashed strawberries
- 2 tablespoons honey

Pour all the ingredients into a food processor and pulse to combine them. Pour the mixture into ice pop molds and freeze them for at least 6 hours. Serve the ice pops right out of the freezer.

## THE RECIPES

——

# DRINKS
## DRINKS
### DRINKS
#### DRINKS
##### DRINKS

There's an old joke about Nashville: it's a drinking town with a music problem. And true, we have a reputation for tears in beers under the neon moons. Walk among the honky-tonks downtown at pretty much any hour, and you'll find music flowing—and the drinks right along with it.

Outside Robert's Western World, there used to be a blackboard sign that read WELCOME TO NASHVILLE. IT'S TIME TO DRINK. And sometimes tourists and locals can't help but oblige. When the Tennessee Titans played the Chicago Bears a couple of years ago, the combination of football fans, country music lovers, and downtown dwellers drank one major honky completely out of domestic beer.

Well before that, in the 1960s and '70s, performers at the Ryman—Patsy Cline, Willie Nelson, Kris Kristofferson, Waylon Jennings, and Roger Miller—used to sneak across the alley for beers at Tootsies between sets. Locals know the back alleys behind the honky-tonks still make the best way to enter the bars, especially on busy nights when lines snake out the front doors.

But it's not just the clang of Miller High Life empties tossed into barroom trash cans that means we've wet our whistles. We're apt to spend evenings with craft cocktails at Patterson House or No. 308 and maybe end the night cracking a PBR. Likewise, we'll revel in the Nashville Symphony before hitting the honky-tonks, going from violin to fiddle in less than one city block.

We also have a rich history of distilling here, with the world's most famous whiskey, Jack Daniel's, just an hour and a half's drive south. Meanwhile in town, Charlie and Andy Nelson have been reviving their family's century-old distilling tradition, which once produced even more whiskey than Jack in its heyday. Others, such as Corsair Distillery, have built a respected reputation for craft and creativity in Triple Smoke Whiskey and Quinoa Whiskey, among other options.

As for beer, our craft scene thrives too, with pioneers of the modern wave of craft brews like Blackstone and Yazoo joined in more recent years by Jackalope, Black Abbey, Little Harpeth, and Tennessee Brew Works. The brewing tradition hearkens back to the late 1800s when breweries like William Gerst Brewing came along. Though Gerst stopped brewing in 1954, Yazoo partnered with the owner of the Gerst Haus restaurant, originally established by the Gerst family, to carry on the name and bring the Gerst amber ale recipe back to Nashville in 2011.

And of course it's not all about the booze. The art of sweet tea is alive and well, as well as fruit tea punch, spiced tea, and coffee. So get ready to pick your favorite elixir, because you'll surely be offered a drink.

## KITCHEN PLAYLIST

In the home of country music, we have plenty of drinking songs to choose from. These feature beverages from whiskey to watermelon wine.

**I Think I'll Just Stay Here and Drink**
MERLE HAGGARD

Released in 1980 on Haggard's album *Back to the Barrooms*, this song hit number one on the country charts.

**Old Dogs, Children, and Watermelon Wine**
TOM T. HALL

This song was inspired by a conversation Hall had with a janitor at a Miami Beach hotel during the 1972 Democratic National Convention.

**Tennessee Whiskey**
GEORGE JONES

He had more than 150 recordings on *Billboard*'s country chart, including one of his most famous, "He Stopped Loving Her Today." But this song compares his lover to that smooth Tennessee whiskey.

**Black Caffeine**
EMMYLOU HARRIS AND RODNEY CROWELL

Harris waited tables and performed folk songs in the 1960s in Greenwich Village. She moved to Nashville in the early 1980s.

# Nelson's Green Brier Distillery

Distillers and brewers keep busy in Nashville, including owners of the Jackalope Brewing Company, who grow hops on a local farm.

At twenty-one years old, Charlie Nelson had already studied and bartended in Paris and traveled throughout Southeast Asia. But he would uncover his greatest discovery a few miles from his Nashville hometown at a Citgo gas station on the way to pick up a quarter of a cow.

Before Prohibition, Charlie's great-great-great-grandfather, Charles Nelson, had operated one of the largest Tennessee whiskey operations. He sold nearly 380,000 gallons in 1885, for example, while a little company called Jack Daniel's had the production capacity of about 23,000 gallons.

So when Charlie, his brother Andy, and his father made a random stop for fuel along Distillery Road, they were bowled over to find a historical marker that led them to the old warehouse that had once held the family business. The butcher who gave them the beef also directed them to a historical center, where a staff member produced two empty bottles from the distillery bearing their name—*Green Brier Handmade Sour Mash Tennessee Whiskey, Chas. Nelson, Distiller, Nashville, Tenn.* Before they left the town, they even drank from the spring that had fed the old still. "Man, this is what we're here to do," Charlie remembers saying. "At that point, everything made sense to me."

And, as a student of humanities and the repeated myths that help form culture, Charlie knew the story hardly started there.

Back in 1850, John Philip Nelson gathered his family aboard the *Helena Sloman* and set sail from their home in Germany to what he hoped would be a better life in America. As family legend goes, he had converted every material possession into gold and created a special suit to hold the bars on his person. So when the ship capsized and he went overboard, he quickly sank. Survivors of the accident included his fifteen-year-old son, Charles.

Arriving in his new country with just the clothes on his back, Charles Nelson had no choice but to work hard. He learned about the soap- and candle-making business and butchery by way of New York and Cincinnati. He landed in Nashville and opened a wholesale grocery on Second Avenue to offer his best products, meats, coffee, and whiskey.

While the grocery's coffeemaker created the Maxwell House brand, Charles Nelson focused his energy on the whiskey. He bought the distillery in Greenbrier that made the whiskey for his store, improved the processes, and soon began to thrive. Among the hundreds of whiskey distilleries in Tennessee at the time, Nelson's was first to sell in a bottle rather than a jug or barrel. When he died in 1891, his wife, Louisa, kept the business running—at least until statewide prohibition shut her down in 1909. She finished selling what the distillery had produced, but unlike Jack Daniel's and George Dickel, she never opened again.

Wind the pocket watch forward a hundred years to 2009. That's the year Charlie Nelson and his brother Andy, still in their twenties, re-formed the company.

"Everybody was really excited for us to start resurrecting it," he says. "But did they believe we'd be able to do it?"

Some members of the Jackalope crew pause for a photo.

The brothers launched Belle Meade Bourbon, the first of several labels under Nelson's Green Brier Distillery, in April 2012. By selling the whiskey produced at another distillery in Lawrenceburg, Indiana, they were able to raise the money they needed for a still, open their own operation in Nashville in 2014, and produce the signature Green Brier label, a true Tennessee whiskey. They even have the original family recipe to work from.

Today, at the heart of their thirty-thousand-square-foot space sits a fifteen-foot copper still that they call Ms. Louisa after their triple-great-grandmother. And to keep himself centered, Charlie said he sometimes reads over the obituary of Charles Nelson, "a man of action" and inclusion who went beyond whiskey to create the first Musical Union in Nashville.

Also inside the distillery hangs a giant American flag. It's a symbol for our country, but it also celebrates the fight for a better life and listening to a calling. Because as the Nelsons stand to prove, those who work hard and chase that American dream will sometimes catch it.

Charlie Nelson (left) and his brother Andy Nelson visit the famly's old barrel house in Greenbrier, Tennessee.

These days, the Nelsons make their whiskey at a distillery in Nashville where Marathon Motorcars were once manufactured.

BELLE MEADE

SOUR MASH
WHISKEY
BOURBON

# The Summer Fling

Samir Osman makes a version of this warm-weather drink with local product. He bartended in New York City and San Francisco before returning home to his native Nashville.

**Makes 1 drink**

| | |
|---|---|
| 3 | strawberries |
| 4 | basil leaves |
| 2 | ounces (60 ml) Belle Meade Bourbon |
| ¾ | ounce lemon juice |
| 1 | teaspoon honey |
| 1 | ounce light lager |

Muddle two of the strawberries and three of the basil leaves in a cocktail shaker. Add the bourbon, lemon juice, and honey. Shake vigorously with ice.

Pour into tumbler. Top the cocktail with the beer. Garnish with the remaining basil leaf and strawberry before serving.

# Winter Whiskey Warmer

Bartender Shannon Melidis created this warming concoction to heat up cold Nashville nights.

**Makes 1 drink**

| | |
|---|---|
| | A few drops Armagnac brandy |
| 2 | ounces (60 ml) rye whiskey |
| ¼ | ounce apple brandy |
| ¼ | ounce spiced simple syrup (see Note) |
| 2 | drops black walnut bitters (such as Fee Brothers brand) |
| | 2-inch (5-cm) piece orange peel |

Place the Armagnac into a chilled double old-fashioned glass and swirl.

In a cocktail shaker filled with ice, stir the rye whiskey, apple brandy, and spiced simple syrup. Strain the mixture into the old-fashioned glass. Drizzle bitters onto the drink, squeeze orange peel over it to disperse the oils, and garnish it with the peel before serving.

*Note:* To make spiced simple syrup, in a small saucepan over medium, combine 1 cup (240 ml) water with 1 cup (200 g) sugar. Add a cinnamon stick, 8 whole cloves, 8 black peppercorns, 6 allspice berries, a ½-inch (12-mm) piece of fresh ginger, and freshly grated nutmeg. Heat until the sugar is dissolved. Remove the syrup from the heat and let it steep about 5 minutes. Strain and refrigerate it until needed. Syrup will keep for up to a month.

# The Papaw

A handful or entire sleeve of gas station peanuts poured directly into a bottle of Coke brings back memories of many grandfathers in the South as well as the working man on the go. Though the origin of this combo for a snack (or meal) is unclear, it makes a salty-sweet treat with a bit of nostalgia. Ben Clemons, bartender and co-owner of No. 308, takes it one brilliant step further by adding bourbon. He insists it isn't a cocktail but an American novelty—aside from the use of Mexican Coke, of course, which is sweetened with cane sugar just as Papaw would probably prefer it.

**Makes 1 drink**

1 (12-ounce/355-ml) bottle Mexican Coke

2 ounces (60 ml) Belle Meade Bourbon

A handful of peanuts

Drink down or reserve a little less than half of the Coke for another use. Add the bourbon to the bottle, followed by the peanuts. Serve with additional peanuts for snacking.

# Holiday Eggnog

This old-fashioned way of making eggnog uses basic ingredients. Choose the best quality ingredients you can, and it will pay off in taste.

**Makes about 6 servings**

12 large eggs, separated

1 quart (960 L) heavy cream

¾ cup (150 g) sugar

6 ounces (180 ml) Belle Meade Bourbon

Freshly grated nutmeg for garnish

In separate bowls, beat the egg yolks well, and beat the whites until stiff peaks form. Also beat the cream until it thickens. Add the sugar to the egg yolks and beat again to combine; beat in the bourbon. Fold together the beaten cream and egg whites. Serve the eggnog with a dusting of freshly grated nutmeg on top.

# Sweet Tea, Honey

On the sweet tea spectrum, this version sits far to the not-as-sweet side. Feel free to add more honey and adjust it to your liking. A touch of baking soda added to tea helps counteract the tea's natural tannins, making for a smoother taste.

**Makes about 10 servings**

- 2 family-size tea bags (or 6 standard-size tea bags)
- ¼ teaspoon baking soda
- ¼ cup (60 ml) honey
- 2 sprigs mint (optional)
- Lemon wedges for serving

In a medium saucepan, bring 3 cups (720 ml) water to a boil. Remove the pan from the heat and add the baking soda. Add the tea bags and allow them to steep for 5 minutes.

Remove the tea bags, stir in the honey, and allow the tea to cool enough to pour into a serving pitcher. Stir in 7 cups (1.7 L) cold water. Taste and adjust the honey if you'd like the tea to be sweeter. Add the mint, if desired.

Serve the tea over ice with lemon wedges as garnish.

# Southern Fruit Tea Punch

Many of Nashville's old-school establishments offer fruit tea blended with lemonade and orange juice concentrate and sometimes even a splash of Sprite. Though these are often served over ice in Styrofoam cups, they're sweet enough for the punch bowl, too—hence the name. This version, made with freshly squeezed juice, is a punch that you don't have to feel guilty about swilling more regularly.

**Makes about 10 servings**

- 2 family-size tea bags (or 6 standard-size tea bags)
- 1 cinnamon stick
- ½ cup (100 g) sugar
- ¾ cup (180 ml) freshly squeezed orange juice
- ¼ cup (60 ml) freshly squeezed lemon juice
- Orange slices for garnish

In a medium saucepan, bring 3 cups (720 ml) water to a boil. Remove the pan from the heat, add the tea bags and cinnamon stick, and allow the mixture to steep for 5 minutes. Remove the tea bags and cinnamon stick and stir in the sugar until it is dissolved.

In a serving pitcher, combine the orange and lemon juices. When the steeped tea is cool enough, pour it into the pitcher. Add 6 cups (1.6 L) cold water. Serve the tea punch over ice with orange slices as garnish.

# Eastside Redeye

This drink is named for East Nashville. It's home to one of the city's most beloved and most unusual festivals with an artistic and bohemian vibe, Tomato Art Fest. Though the festival started as a tomato-themed art show at Art & Invention Gallery, it has morphed into a neighborhood-wide event with the Second Line Parade, featuring neighbors in tomato costumes and beehive hairdos, as well as contests for haiku writing, Bloody Mary recipes, best redhead, ugliest tomato, and more.

Though the Eastside redeye might look similar to a Bloody Mary, it has a lighter, cleaner taste, with the effervescence of beer, a bright squeeze of lemon, and the clean taste of tomato juice. A pinch of cayenne pepper in the salted rim gives the lips a tingle. It's a refreshing sip you might need on a hot day—or the day after.

**Makes 1 drink**

*For the salt rim:*
- Juice of 2 lemons
- 2 tablespoons salt
- 1 teaspoon celery seeds
- Pinch of cayenne pepper

*For the drink:*
- 2 ounces (60 ml) tomato juice
- A few shakes cayenne hot pepper sauce
- 2 shakes Worcestershire sauce
- 1 (12-ounce/355-ml) can lager beer
- Celery stalk for garnish
- Lemon wedge for garnish

*Make the salt rim:*
Pour the lemon juice into a small bowl. In a separate shallow dish, combine the salt, celery seeds, and cayenne. Dip the rim of a tall pint glass into the lemon juice and then into the salt mixture giving it a turn to coat.

*Make the drink:*
Pour the tomato juice into the glass, add the hot sauce and Worcestershire, and fill it with beer. You might need to give it a few stirs with a spoon.

Garnish with a celery stalk and a lemon wedge before serving.

# Basil Lemonade

Tennesseans with even the smallest of herb gardens know it's a good idea to have scads of recipes for fragrant summertime basil when it thrives.

Susannah Fotopulos of the gardening nonprofit Plant the Seed once took a bunch as a gift to friends, and they didn't waste a single second, making use of it by dunking it in the after-dinner hot tea, much as you might use mint.

For a cooler take, I like the proportions for this lemonade, which makes it less sweet and more on the tart and tingly side. I also recommend making this lemonade in a pitcher and pouring it over ice. Adding ice to the mix before serving it runs the risk of watering it down too much.

2 **(750-ml) bottles mineral water, one or both sparkling**

**About 1 cup (240 ml) fresh lemon juice**

**About 1¼ cups (300 ml) basil simple syrup (see Note)**

**Basil leaves for garnish**

Pour the mineral water into a medium to large pitcher. Then add the lemon juice and basil simple syrup. Taste and adjust the proportions as you wish. Refrigerate the lemonade until you are ready to serve it poured over ice and garnished with basil leaves.

*Note:* To make the basil simple syrup, in a small saucepan, combine 2 cups (480 ml) water with 2 cups (80 g) basil and 1 cup (200 g) sugar and simmer until the sugar is dissolved, about 5 minutes. Remove the syrup from the heat and let it cool. Strain it into an airtight container and store it in the refrigerator for up to a week.

# A Float Named Sue

It's appropriate that a beer named Sue made by the local brewery Yazoo should be dressed in a black label like the man, Johnny Cash. This rich, smoky beer also plays a key role in my favorite ice cream at Jeni's Splendid Ice Creams. The Ohio-based shop with a James Beard award–winning owner opened its first location outside its home state in East Nashville. A line formed quickly out the door, and it seems to have stayed that way since. The ice cream called Yazoo Sue with Rosemary Beer Nuts inspired this deconstructed float version of that treat. The beer has a bitter nip that helps take the sweet edge off the ice cream and syrupy nuts. Chocolate, vanilla, and rosemary are like the June Carter to the beer's Johnny Cash.

**Makes 4 floats**

*For the wet pecans:*

- ½ cup (50 g) pecans, broken into pieces
- ½ cup (120 ml) light corn syrup
- 1 teaspoon vanilla extract
- ½ teaspoon fresh rosemary, chopped
- ⅛ teaspoon salt

*For the floats:*

- 8 big scoops vanilla ice cream
- ¼ cup (60 ml) chocolate syrup
- 1 (750-milliliter) bottle or 2 (12-ounce/355-ml) bottles Yazoo SUE beer

  Whipped cream for garnish

Rinse four pint glasses with water and place them in the freezer so they'll turn frosty.

*Prepare the wet nuts:*
In a saucepan, combine the pecans, corn syrup, vanilla, rosemary, and salt and heat the mixture over low for just a few minutes, until it is warm and soupy. Remove it from the heat and allow it to cool completely.

*Prepare the floats:*
In each glass, begin with a scoop of ice cream, top it with about ½ tablespoon each of chocolate and nuts, followed by a second scoop of ice cream and another spoonful each of chocolate and nuts. Pour the beer over the ice cream until the glass is nearly full. Garnish the floats with whipped cream and a final drizzle of chocolate before serving.

# Index

# *Acknowledgments*

**T**his section has just one song in its playlist: "Thank You for a Life," by Kris Kristofferson, with gratitude for opportunities given. And if I could, I would belt it out to all the people who have helped make this book happen.

For the chances in particular, I'm thankful for my agent Sally Ekus, who has offered unwavering encouragement and positivity, as well as editor Holly Dolce, for giving me the opportunity and direction to write a book that was more than I imagined. I'm appreciative of many others at Abrams, from the editors to the artists who helped shepherd this project along, including Camaren Subhiyah, Michael Clark, Sarah Massey, and designer Deb Wood.

Thank you to photographer Andrea Behrends, who bravely took this project on when neither of us had worked on a cookbook before, and thanks to Hannah Messinger, the food stylist who cooked, cleaned, and beautified all while keeping the studio vibe mellow. Miranda Whitcomb Pontes and Coco, thank you for generously allowing us to take over your light-filled and chic home for several days as our studio.

To the Southern Foodways Alliance family, I'm forever grateful for your work, inspiration, and support. A special shout-out goes to Sheri Castle, who looked over many of these recipes. Thanks also to John T. Edge, Ann Egerton, and the late John Egerton for lighting the paths of so many. SFA oral histories, films, and meals have informed this project, as have talks from podiums and conversations around late-night fires.

Thank you to the many friends mentioned throughout this book for graciously sharing your stories and recipes. There are too many of you to name on this page, so I'm going to throw you a party.

Thank you to Erin Byers Murray and Cindy Wall for the moral support and healthy creative distraction. Thanks also to the tribe members who let me cook in their kitchens. Ann Manning, Jaime Miller, Leigh Griggs, and Jessica Doyle, thank you for chopping carrots and offering feedback, often while raising a glass.

I'm thankful that my grandmother's skillet can be found on several pages of this book, and special gratitude goes out to my mother and father, who turned out to be the most meticulous recipe testers I've ever known.

To my fiancé Tony, thank you for keeping me laughing, loved, and inspired. During the trial and error of recipe development, I'm glad you never complained when dinner consisted of deviled eggs with chocolate pound cake.

Finally to Nashville, thank you the most. As new restaurants open and condos go up, I'm glad to see you fighting for the history and tradition that made this place in its physical form, but I'm most happy to see you working to keep this the open and hospitable city that drew so many of us here in the first place. I'm grateful that you welcomed me here many years ago, and I'm proud to call you home.

GONE TOMORROW LAMBCHOP W

FISH AND WHISTLE JOHN PRIN

PRAY FOR THE FISH RANDY TRAV

WAGON FARMER'S BLUES MARTY

CHET ATKINS PLAY IT LOUD, RA

HIGHWATER MY OLD FRIEND JAC

SWEET DREAMS JIM OBLON CO

ON ME KENNY VAUGHAN THE BI

CANDY MARION JAMES MONEY M

PIE BOB DYLAN I THINK I'LL JUS

HAGGARD OLD DOGS, CHILDR

TOM T. HALL TENNESSEE WI

CAFFEINE EMMYLOU HARRIS AND R